CELEBRATING
AVRAHAM

CELEBRATING AVRAHAM

Avraham Biran
The Excavator of Dan at 90

BIBLICAL ARCHAEOLOGY SOCIETY
WASHINGTON, DC

Library of Congress Cataloging-in-Publication Data

Celebrating Avraham : Avraham Biran, the excavator of Dan at 90.
p. cm.
Reprints of articles and photographs of Avraham Biran, and his archaeological digs and discoveries.
Includes bibliographical references.
ISBN 1-880317-56-7 (pbk.)
1. Excavations (Archaeology)—Israel—Dan (Extinct city) 2. Dan (Extinct city) 3. Biran, Avraham
Interviews.
DS110.D33C45   1999
   933—dc21   99-41972
                                                          CIP

©1999
Biblical Archaeology Society
4710 41st Street, NW
Washington, DC 20016

Reprinted from *Biblical Archaeology Review*
Chapter 1: September/October 1999
Chapter 2: July/August 1987
Chapter 3: September/October 1981
Chapter 4: November/December 1984
Chapter 5: January/February 1989
Chapter 6: March/April 1994, September/October 1994
Chapter 7: September/October 1998
Chapter 8: July/August 1994
Chapter 9: March/April 1983

Front cover: Photograph by David Harris, Jerusalem.
Back cover: Upper right photograph by the Israel Museum, Jerusalem, collection of the
Israel Antiquities Authority; all others by Zev Radovan, Jerusalem.

CELEBRATING AVRAHAM

CONTENTS

CELEBRATING AVRAHAM

FOREWORD

All of us at Hebrew Union College–Jewish Institute of Religion join in saluting Dr. Avraham Biran as he celebrates his 90th birthday. The publication of this volume in his honor is testimony to the profound impact Dr. Biran has had in his life—both as an archaeologist, in the world of scholarship and research, and as a leader of the people and the State of Israel. His influence is worldwide and yet, at the same time, personal and embracing. His human touch is as grand as his intellectual scope and near limitless achievements.

Dr. Biran was appointed director of the Nelson Glueck School of Biblical Archaeology of the Hebrew Union College–Jewish Institute of Religion in Jerusalem upon his retirement as director of the Israel Department of Antiquities and Museums. In the quarter of a century since then, his career has been one of extraordinary service, marked by his excavations at Aroer, Ira, Yesud Hama'alah, Anathoth and Tel Dan, by his teaching, lecturing and publishing, and by his continuing leadership in every aspect of the work of the College–Institute. Building on the achievements of the past, he has placed the school at the center of the intellectual and academic world, not only in Israel, but worldwide. His advice, counsel and personal guidance have blessed the leadership of the school, as well as the faculty and students. His vision, sensitivity, excitement and commitment have transformed all our work.

To him and his beloved wife, Ruth, we extend wishes of continuing fulfillment and blessing—*Ad meah v'esrim*—may he reach the proverbial 120 years of promise and blessing, filling each moment to the brim.

Rabbi Sheldon Zimmerman, President
Rabbi Michael Marmur, Dean of the Jerusalem School
August 1999

CELEBRATING AVRAHAM

PREFACE

Avraham Biran is, quite simply, the world's most popular lecturer on Biblical archaeology (although his friend and colleague Trude Dothan is a very close second). I know this because he has, as have hundreds of other scholars, lectured for us at seminars sponsored by the Biblical Archaeology Society. At the end of each seminar, the audience gives us evaluations of the lecturers. Invariably, he receives rave reviews.

I mention this not because this is such an impressive mountain to climb (although it is), but because the reasons tell us so much about the man. He is full of energy and enthusiasm. His stentorian voice is not intimidating, but engaging. He obviously loves—and knows—his subject. Yet he invariably ends his lectures with questions he cannot answer, puzzles he has not solved. There is always more to learn. His conclusions are provisional. Maybe next year will surprise us, he says. He is therefore tentative, tolerant of other views. For Avraham, there is always next season.

Yet—I have to say it—he is also lucky. How else to explain the stream of startling finds that have come year after year from this pile of dirt we call Tel Dan? He himself would say, as he does at the end of the interview that forms the first chapter of this book, that there is someone up there with a long white beard who is looking after him. Perhaps he is right.

As an archaeologist, Avraham Biran is swimming against the stream. He knows this. It is because he is willing to call himself a Biblical archaeologist. He will openly tell you of his interest in, indeed his love for, the Bible and the land in which it was written. He candidly admits that he looks to archaeology to help him understand it better. This is not always a popular stance among younger archaeologists or among Bible scholars who have recently been tagged "Biblical minimalists," scholars who deny that there is any history in the Bible. That is why in our interview Avraham prefaces his remarks about a passage from the Bible that his excavation at Dan has illuminated with the statement, "You can use that against me." But it is a matter of principle with him. He knows who he is.

Given the publicity his life has brought him, you might suppose that he welcomes the limelight, but this is not true. Not that he shuns it—but he is simply indifferent to it. He is willing to be interviewed; he will be open and candid; but he does not seek attention, and he frequently expresses his doubts that people will be interested in him. Once we get started, however, he brings to it the same energy and enthusiasm he brings to everything in his life. At one o'clock I suggest we break for lunch. He does not have lunch, he says. Hanni Hirsch, his longtime assistant, brings him a cup of coffee and cookies. At four, Hanni comes in again and says we should stop for the day. (After all, Biran is going to be 90, and I am tired from concentrating the entire day.) "No, no, let's go on!" says Avraham. We do. By five, Hanni has gone home. Let's stop now, I say. "Another ten minutes," says Avraham. We're planning to continue tomorrow anyway, so we stop, even though Avraham shows no sign of flagging. I leave. And he continues to work.

I vividly remember the calls from Israel six years ago as the word spread like wildfire that Biran had uncovered an inscription with the words *Beth David*, "House of David," in it, the first time the name David had been found outside the Bible. I immediately called him (he didn't call me). I finally convinced him to allow me to let some of my friends in the media know about it. As a result, a story appeared on the front page of the *New York Times* and in *Time* magazine. Naturally, I also asked Avraham to write a story on the inscription for *Biblical Archaeology Review*. He didn't want to do that because he had already written a scholarly article on it that anyone who was interested could consult. He didn't want to rehash what he had already said (together with colleague Joseph Naveh) in the *Israel Exploration Journal* (whose circulation is approximately three percent of *BAR*'s). I felt a responsibility to tell our readers about this astounding find. So Avraham said he would write a more general article for *BAR* on the many inscriptions that had been found at Dan. I agreed, asking only that he give special attention to the *Beth David* inscription.

His manuscript arrived and went through our usual intensive editing process during which I added a punchy opening paragraph that read like this: "It's not often that an archaeological find makes the front page of the *New York Times* (to say nothing of *Time* magazine). But that's what happened last summer to a discovery at Tel Dan ..."

Avraham objected to the opening. It seemed to him bragging. He feared it would indicate he was happy with, may even have sought, this kind of media coverage. It was not his way. He would begin pedestrianly: "In the 27th season of the excavation of Tel Dan, an inscription was discovered ..." I, of course, was reluctant to lose the chance for such a great opening, and his objection came so late in the publication process and required such rearrangement that we finally agreed that instead of his name appearing as the author of the article, we would state it was based on the scientific report in the *Israel Exploration Journal* "and on other materials supplied by Professor Biran." That is why the article that forms Chapter 6 in this book technically has no author. It is, however, his work.

Of course, I was wrong for insisting, although I hope some of you may agree that it is a harmless opening. But my point is neither one nor the other. I think the episode betrays both Avraham's indifference to the publicity that is often showered upon him and his scholarly integrity. As a matter of principle, he is going to uphold the standards that he believes scholars should live by.

I hasten to add that, typically, this episode did not mar in the least our warm personal relationship. He recognizes his obligation to the public and gladly works with me to meet that obligation in so many ways—in his publications, in his many lectures to both popular and scholarly audiences that the Biblical Archaeology Society has arranged over the years, in his interviews and in his willingness to share his vast knowledge with all who approach him.

I want to conclude with one final aspect of Avraham's character that may be related to his indifference to publicity, and this surely comes through in the interviews in this book. That is his complete lack of pretense, his openness, his essential humanity, his willingness to be himself. He is not trying to create any predetermined impression. There he is—the man—take it or leave it.

And there we have it. We take it and we love it. And we love him. *Ad meah v'esrim*! To 120!

Hershel Shanks
Washington, D.C.
July 1999

CELEBRATING AVRAHAM

THANKS

Only with their generous support has this tribute
to Avraham Biran been possible:

Richard and Joan Scheuer

⮜⬥⮞

We were first alerted to Avraham's impending birthday by my dear friend Michael Klein, former dean of the HUC Jerusalem school, so it all started with Michael. HUC President, Rabbi Sheldon Zimmerman, and Rabbi Michael Marmur, dean of the Jerusalem school, have been most cooperative in working out arrangements for the publication and production of this book.

Hanni Hirsch, Avraham Biran's longtime assistant at the college and a member of the excavation staff since 1974, gathered photographs, answered last-minute questions and always knew when to tell Avraham to let his tired interviewer go home.

David Harris of Jerusalem captured the spirit and essence of Avraham in the photographs taken during the interview that forms Chapter 1. Zev Radovan's photos of the tell, the artifacts and the archaeologists bring to life 34 years of excavation at Dan, as do the images by George Kelm, John Laughlin, Garo Nalbandian, Duby Tal and the Israel Museum.

Design director Robert Sugar, with David Fox and Robin Cather of AURAS Design, transformed the disparate chapters into a breathtakingly beautiful book.

The staff of the Biblical Archaeology Society was a critical element in the creation of this book, especially *Bible Review* managing editor Molly Dewsnap, who meticulously and creatively managed the editorial production. John Goltz and Bonnie Mullin painstakingly corrected the text. The overall project was under the supervision of BAS executive director Bridget Young. Lauren Krause and Angela Botzer directed the production of the book.

To all, my deep gratitude.

Hershel Shanks
Washington, D.C.
July 1999

CHAPTER ONE

In this interview from April 1999, Avraham Biran reminisces about growing up in Palestine, falling in love with archaeology (and his wife) as a young student in the United States and returning home to a life divided between the government and the tell. It is a story peopled by some of the greatest archaeologists and Bible scholars of the past century—and Biran stands among them.

The Excavator of Dan Recalls Growing Up in Pre-State Israel, Great Archaeologists He's Known and Why He's a Biblical Archaeologist

Biran at

On October 23, 1999, Avraham Biran, director of the Nelson Glueck School of Biblical Archaeology at Hebrew Union College in Jerusalem, will celebrate his 90th birthday. He will also have completed his 34th season at Tel Dan, the longest-running archaeological excavation in Israel.

He has led an extraordinary life—as a student, a government official, a diplomat, a dedicated Zionist and, not least, a Bible scholar and archaeologist. His life has stretched over most of the history of modern archaeology in the Holy Land, and he has known and worked with the leading men and women who participated in that history.

The presidency of the Israel Exploration Society is a largely honorary position. For many years it was held by Benjamin Mazar, the doyen of Biblical archaeologists. Since Mazar's death in 1995, the position had remained vacant—until this year, when Avraham Biran was named to the post. May he serve for many years to come.

The following interview by BAR editor Hershel Shanks was conducted in Biran's Jerusalem office on April 13 and 14, 1999.

Hershel Shanks: The first scientific excavation in Palestine occurred in 1890, as you know. Sir William Matthew Flinders Petrie dug at Tel el-Hesi.

Avraham Biran: That's right.

You were born 19 years later.
Yes—in 1909.

In a way, you're the last living link to that past—between the beginning of scientific archaeology in this land and Biblical archaeology today. You knew Petrie, didn't you?

Yes, when I graduated with a Ph.D. from Johns Hopkins, I became the Thayer Fellow at the American School of Oriental Research in Jerusalem, now the William F. Albright School of Archaeological Research. That was in 1935, during the Depression, and the fellowship didn't pay anything.

It was just an honor. I held it for two years, and I can boast that I am the oldest living Thayer Fellow. So it was worth something. But I did get a room to live in at the school, and my room was next to the room of Sir Flinders and Lady Petrie.

Were you a bachelor then?
Yes, but then I married. In 1936 my girlfriend, Ruth, came over from America, and we got married. She, too, lived at the school. She became the school secretary. The great William Foxwell Albright was the director. When he left, Nelson Glueck became the director.

Ninety

Was Petrie already Sir Flinders at that time?

Oh, yes. I remember him sitting in the garden of the school for afternoon tea. He was very amiable and had a wonderful smile—all benevolence, very kind. We used to sit and chat and drink tea. He had a long white beard. He died when he was almost 90, just as I am now. To me any gentleman with a white beard was an old man. I didn't think then about when I would get to be old. I remember he had difficulty hearing in one ear. He told me—I'm quoting him, I'm not being unkind—that he turns his deaf ear when Lady Petrie speaks! He was very human.

That was in 1936, when the "disturbances" broke out.

The Arabs attacked Jewish settlements because the British government had allowed some Jewish immigration into Palestine. It lasted until 1939. The Jewish population complained to the British that they were not strict enough with the rioting Arabs. We were talking about the disturbances, and Petrie came up with an idea. He said, "You know the trouble in the Middle East is not political. The trouble in the Middle East is the goat." The goat eats everything. Unlike sheep, goats eat all kinds of grass. They even eat from the trees; they eat the bark so the tree dies. Petrie said they were doing that all over the Middle East. He said eliminate the goat and then the fields will blossom and there will be greenery all around and there will be no reason for disturbances.

He was very much admired, and he was always the center of attention. We all enjoyed being with him.

He was supposed to be stingy—he wouldn't spend money.

I'm not sure it was he as much as she. The story goes—whether it's true or apocryphal, I don't know—that when Lady Petrie would organize an expedition to an excavation, she'd invite all the people who wanted to come and join his staff and put them around the table and give them food. And the story goes that Lady Petrie would choose those who ate the least.

Were you born in Palestine?

Yes, I call myself a Mayflower Israeli. My great-grandfather established the village of Rosh Pina in Galilee. So I consider myself a Galilean.

Where did he come from?

From Romania, in the 1880s, during the wave of Zionist immigration of Hovevei Tzion, "the lovers of Zion," who came to settle the land. My great-great uncle, a man named David Shub, was sent as an advance party to see where he could buy some land. The Jews of Safed owned a piece of land next to an Arab village. The Jews of Safed apparently weren't good farmers and couldn't make a go of it, so when my great-great uncle came here, he bought the land from the Jews of Safed for a new village. And they called it Rosh Pina, "*Even ma-asu ha-bonim haitah l'rosh pinah*," from the Book of Psalms, "The stone that the builders rejected became the *rosh pina*, the corner stone."

In the early 1900s it was difficult for people to make a living in Rosh Pina, so my father went down to Egypt to look for work. In those days in Egypt foreign companies owned large tracts of land that grew cotton. My father, who they knew had come from a family of colonists, was put in charge of a village of cotton workers. When he decided to get married, he came back to Palestine to look for a bride. He started in Rosh Pina in the north and worked his way south. When he got to Petah Tikva [near Tel Aviv], he met a very beautiful young woman who was a teacher in the local school. I guess they fell in love, because they decided to get married. Then he took her with him to Egypt. But my mother said that if she is going to have children, she wanted to have them back home. So she came back. That's where my sister and I were born. That was in the days of the Turks; the Ottoman Empire was ruling here. So we had Ottoman citizenship. Later, when the British passed the law of citizenship, the most coveted status was Turkish. And those who had Turkish citizenship automatically became Palestinians. We were all Ottoman—like the Mayflower.

Biran—Nine Decades

1909	Born to Aharon and Naomi Bergman
1926	Graduates Reali High School, Haifa
1928	Teacher's Diploma, David Yellin Teachers Seminary, Jerusalem
1928-30	Teacher, Reali Elementary School, Haifa
1930-31	Student, University of Pennsylvania
1935	Ph.D., Johns Hopkins University, Phi Beta Kappa
1936	Marries Ruth Frankel
1935-37	Thayer Fellow, American School of Oriental Research, Jerusalem; excavates at Ras el-Kharrubeh; Tel Jerishe, near Tel Aviv; Tell el-Kheleifeh, near Aqaba; Irbid, Jordan; Tepe Gaura, near Mosul; and Khafaje, near Baghdad.
1937-45	District Officer, Beth-Shean Valley, Government of Palestine
1946	District Officer, Jerusalem, Government of Palestine
1948	Deputy Military Governor, Jerusalem, Government of Israel
1949-55	District Commissioner, Jerusalem, Government of Israel
1951-	Chairman, Israel Government Names Committee
1955-58	Consul-General of Israel for 11 western states, Los Angeles
1958-61	Director, Armistice Affairs, Jerusalem
1961-74	Director, Israel Department of Antiquities and Museums
1966-	Begins excavations at Tel Dan
1974-	Director, Nelson Glueck School of Biblical Archaeology, Hebrew Union College-Jewish Institute of Religion, Jerusalem; continues excavations at Tel Dan; directs excavations at Ira and Aroer, in the Negev; Yesud Hamaalah, in Galilee; and Anathoth, near Jerusalem
1978-	Chairman, Israel Exploration Society
1999	President, Israel Exploration Society

What language did you first learn as a child?

My mother spoke to us in Hebrew. But in school in Egypt, I studied Arabic, French, Italian and English as a child of six, seven, eight years old. I remember that if you made a mistake, you stretched out your hands and you got caned. Nobody resented or minded that, I suppose.

My father died in 1919. I remember him lying in bed, probably with pneumonia. I don't know what kind of medical care there was at the time in Mansura, Egypt, where we lived. My mother found a young doctor fresh from Paris. He did something to my father, put something in his throat. My mother always claimed that killed him, whatever new thing it was.

When my father died, my mother decided to come back to Palestine for good—to Rosh Pina. In those days Rosh Pina had an excellent elementary school, established by people like Itzhaq Epstein, educators of the old school. Something indicative of the times: We had a teacher who taught us Arabic, but he also taught Hebrew to the children of the Arab village next door. Chaim Keller was his name. I still remember him, a wonderful teacher.

ALL-STAR LINEUP. Avraham Biran stands at far right in a group portrait taken in 1935 at the American School of Oriental Research, in Jerusalem. Other notables include the illustrious William Foxwell Albright (fourth from left in the far back row), under whom Biran received his Ph.D. at Johns Hopkins and after whom the school in Jerusalem is today named. Mrs. Albright sits at far left. Clarence Fisher, who led a University of Chicago excavation team at Megiddo, stands third from left in the middle row (with handkerchief in pocket).

Biran, then still known as Bergman, was just beginning a two-year stint as a Thayer Fellow at the American School. In the years that lay ahead, he would work with or meet most of the leading excavators in Near Eastern archaeology.

One of the teachers, who came from Russia, played the violin. He decided that we must have a choir. My mother, like every good Jewish mother, thought her children could do everything, and she said, "Well, you should be in the choir." Now, I don't have an ear for music. I cannot carry a tune. The teacher said, "Look, I'll try you anyway." So he played the violin, and I was supposed to sing. Of course, I didn't carry the tune and he said no, I couldn't join the choir. I came back and told my mother. She said, "He doesn't know anything. You should be in the choir." A typical Jewish mother. I was 10 or 11 at the time—about 1920.

When I graduated from the elementary school in Rosh Pina, the next question was where I would go to high school. The Eton of Palestine in those days was the Reali school in Haifa. My mother wanted her children to have the best, so we moved to Haifa. It was an excellent school.

We used to do a lot of hiking in those days, and we'd take sandwiches with us. We had a gymnastics teacher—a short fellow, I can still see him—who would get furious if someone left a piece of bread from a sandwich. He would say, "You boys and girls don't know what it was like. I was in the World War [One]. There was famine all over Europe, and you're throwing away a piece of bread." To this day, I cannot throw away a piece of bread. These things stay with you.

Petrie

William Flinders Petrie (1853-1942) pioneered the field of scientific archaeology in the Near East. At 27, he began the first accurate survey of the pyramids of Giza; at 30, he excavated sites in the Nile Delta. His excavation technique was based on the concept that ancient remains lie in strata and that pottery, whose style evolves over time, could be used to date the strata in which it was found. Of particular note was his work at el-Amarna, where he discovered portions of Pharaoh Akhenaten's palace and the el-Amarna tablets, which chronicled dealings between Akhenaten and foreign monarchs. In 1890 he turned his spade to Palestine. His excavation of Tell el-Hesi was the first scientific excavation in the Holy Land. He later excavated Tell Jemmeh, Tell el-'Ajjul and Tell el-Far'ah South. His archaeological achievements led to his being knighted in 1923.

Albright

William F. Albright (1891-1971) is regarded as the father of modern Biblical archaeology. His careful stratigraphic excavation of Tell Beit Mirsim—a relatively unimportant site—made it the type-site for Palestinian pottery chronology. He and his colleagues believed in the general historical accuracy of the Bible, and he hoped to use archaeological evidence to date the patriarchal narratives. From 1929 until his retirement in 1958, Albright was chair of the Oriental Seminary at Johns Hopkins University; from 1930 to 1968 he edited the *Bulletin of the American Schools of Oriental Research*. Albright cofounded, with David Noel Freedman, the Anchor Bible Series. He is the author of *From the Stone Age to Christianity* (1940) and *Yahweh and the Gods of Canaan* (1968), among many other works.

Glueck

Nelson Glueck (1900-1971), a student of Albright's, was an archaeologist, a Bible scholar and a rabbi. Ordained at Hebrew Union College, he began teaching there in 1929. After working with Albright at Tell Beit Mirsim, Glueck unearthed the Nabatean temple at Jebel el-Tannur in 1937. The following year he excavated the Iron Age site of Tell el-Kheleifeh, which he identified as Solomon's seaport Ezion-Geber. During the Second World War, Glueck worked in Palestine for the U.S. Office of Strategic Services, the forerunner of the CIA, locating water sources in the event of a Nazi invasion. In 1947 he was elected president of Hebrew Union College, and in 1960, he established the college's Biblical and Archaeological School in Jerusalem. Perhaps Glueck's most important archaeological contributions are his still useful survey reports from Transjordan (where he identified more than a thousand sites—most of which were previously unknown) and the Negev (more than 500 sites).

Anyway, we did a lot of hiking. It was not like today, when you go by bus.

If you would ask me where my interest in archaeology started, it was on a hike to Samaria in 1923 or 1924. I was 14. I still remember the columns with the capitals on top. I took a picture of a capital with my little girlfriend beside it.

When I was 13, my mother needed an operation. Again, the same story: They wanted a good doctor. So she went to Tiberias for the operation. She died on the operating table. So here we were, three orphans—my sister and I and my kid brother, who was only five or six years old.

Were you bar mitzvahed at 13?

Well, as an orphan, you don't have very much of a bar mitzvah. My uncle took me to the synagogue. I laid *tefillin* [phylacteries] and read the Torah portion, but it wasn't such a big ceremony like today. My family, of course, was very religious, and my grandmother kept very strictly kosher. We went to *shul* [synagogue], but we didn't have a big do for my bar mitzvah. I don't think any of my friends did either.

My sister and I continued at the Reali school. The principal was very fond of us. In those days high school was four years. The principal had just opened up

a boarding school for the Reali, and he made me a counselor. My sister and I lived at the boarding school.

You never know what will happen to you in this life. Among the students at that time were the children of the Schimmel family in Philadelphia. Herb, the oldest boy, was in my class, and we were very friendly. Years later, in 1930, when I decided to go to study in America, I was accepted at the University of

Pennsylvania in Philadelphia, where Herb and his family lived. So I wrote him a letter saying I was coming to Philadelphia, so of course, the first home I had in Philadelphia was the Schimmel home. When Mrs. Schimmel saw me, she said, "Well, what are you going to do? How are you going to earn a living?" I said, "Well, I'm a licensed teacher." By then I had finished teacher's training college. Unlike people who were teaching Hebrew who just knew the language, I was a trained teacher. I had not only finished a seminar at the teacher's training college, I had taught for two years at the Reali. So Mrs. Schimmel said, "You know, maybe you could teach at a Sunday school." I said, "I'd love to." So she called Rabbi Arnoff, who had a congregation in Camden, New Jersey, just on the other side of the river from Philadelphia. She told him that she had this Palestinian boy here who needed a job. "Don't you know we're in a Depression!" he said. "We don't have jobs, and we don't have any money. Impossible!" But she said, "See him anyway."

So I took a bus and the ferry and I came to the synagogue and I knocked on his door and opened it. He gives me a look and says, "It's you!"

It turns out Rabbi Arnoff was one of three American students who came to study at the Hebrew University [in Jerusalem] when it opened in 1925. And he and I used to study a *daf* [page of the] Talmud every evening. "I'll find you a job!" he said. And I became a teacher at the Camden Hebrew School—all this because the Schimmel family sent their children to the Reali school in Haifa.

Albright knew so much. It was our tota

Anyway, after the Reali the principal said to me, "You will go to Jerusalem to study at the Yellin Teachers Seminary. There you will get your degree as a teacher, and then you will come back and teach at the Reali." That's what I did. In 1928, after the teachers seminary, I went back to Haifa and taught at the Reali for two years in one of the elementary classes. Among my pupils was Ezer Weizman [now president of Israel]. To this day, when I

I went by boat, from Haifa to Marseilles, from Marseilles by train to Cherbourg, and from Cherbourg by boat to New York.

Where did you get the money?

As a teacher at the Reali, I made eight pounds a month. That was a lot of money in those days. I could save half of it.

When we landed in New York, everybody was taken to Ellis Island, even stu-

asked was, "How are you going to live?" That I anticipated. I said, "My uncle, who is a high official in the Palestine government (he was a district officer in Nazareth and in Safed), is going to send me money." You couldn't say you were going to work because that was against all the rules. And then there was one man on the panel who I later learned was a Lebanese American. That was in 1930, after the riots of 1929, when Jews were

despair. He was a genius, and we were just human beings.

see him he calls me *mori*, "my teacher."

After spending two years teaching at the Reali, I decided that I wanted to see the world. I spoke to Arthur Biram, our headmaster. He said the only place to study was Berlin. He was a student of Eduard Meyer, the great historian and Bible scholar. Germany had the top institutions of learning in those days. "But," he said, "there is a beginning of Nazism in Germany, and I don't think you as a Palestinian Jew would enjoy Berlin." Then he said, "Why don't you go to America? You can make a living there. You can teach Hebrew. There are enough Jews there you could teach Hebrew."

So I decided to go to America. I didn't know which university I should go to, so I sent letters to different universities—Columbia, Chicago, Pennsylvania, California.

The first letter of acceptance was from the University of Pennsylvania, so I went to Philadelphia. If I had received the first letter from another school, maybe my whole career would have been different.

DEDICATING THE JERUSALEM CAMPUS of Hebrew Union College in 1960, Biran speaks as archaeologist Nelson Glueck, Israeli diplomat Abba Eban and Ruth Biran sit to his right at the head table. Hebrew Union College (HUC) was founded in 1875 in Cincinnati as the seminary of the Reform movement within Judaism. Today it has branches in New York and Los Angeles, in addition to the Jerusalem school. Glueck was for decades a professor of archaeology at HUC, and Biran credits him with igniting Biran's passion for archaeology. In a fitting turn of events, in 1974 Biran was named head of HUC's Nelson Glueck School of Biblical Archaeology.

dents. We were in this huge hall; I didn't know what to do or what would happen. I saw some guy walking around, and I said to him, "What goes on?" He said, "They can keep you here weeks before they let you in!" So I said, "What happens?" He said, "Well, there is a committee of five people standing like a court. And they ask you questions. After you finish answering, they decide whether you can come into America or not." And a thought occurred to me, something that I have tried to tell my children and grandchildren as a lesson in life. I said to myself, "What questions can they ask?" I walked to a corner and figured out any number of questions. And 90 percent of the questions that they asked me, I had anticipated. There were five people—I can still see their faces—and they started asking questions. One of the questions they

attacked going to the Wailing Wall. This man turned to me and said, "Why is there trouble between the Arabs and the Jews?" That question I did not anticipate; I didn't think they would ask a political question. So I said, "There are hotheads on both sides, and that's what caused all the trouble." He nodded and seemed satisfied with that. And I was allowed in.

What did you study at Penn?

I took undergraduate courses. One of my classmates at the Reali had been David Magnes, the son of Judah Magnes, the first president of the Hebrew University. When I came to Jerusalem to the teachers seminary, I visited David Magnes, and his father asked me, "How will you make a living?" I said, "Well, I will teach Hebrew." It so happened that the Magneses' next-door neighbor was Henrietta

Szold [the founder of Hadassah], from Baltimore. Her niece from Baltimore, named Harriet Levine, came to visit her. Magnes thought Harriet should learn Hebrew, so I gave her private lessons, and Harriet and I became very friendly. Years later, when I was in Philadelphia studying at the University of Pennsylvania, David Magnes's brother Jonathan came to visit and one day suggested, "Let's go visit Harriet in Baltimore." So we went to Baltimore, and that is how I established contact with her. It was Harriet who told me, "Why don't you go to see [William Foxwell] Albright at Johns Hopkins?"

Why did she tell you to go see Albright?

I was interested in the Bible and the history and the geography of the land. Albright had just been made chairman of the Department of Oriental Studies. So I went to see Albright. I don't think he had many students in those days. And here was this Palestinian fellow who spoke Hebrew, who spoke Arabic, who knew the Bible, so he said, "Come and study with me." He gave me a scholarship. One advantage of going to Hopkins was that you could go to graduate school without a B.A.; here was an opportunity. So the next year I left Pennsylvania and went to Baltimore.

What was your impression of Albright?

Albright was a towering figure. He knew so much that it was our total despair. He made us take courses which I think to this day are utterly impossible; you couldn't study all that and know it all. He taught us cuneiform. He taught us hieroglyphics. There was a professor of Sanskrit at Johns Hopkins, a Professor Dumont, and Dumont didn't have any students, so Albright said to us, "You take Sanskrit."

When Hitler became chancellor of Germany and the Jewish professors felt they were going to be expelled, Albright extended an invitation to Professor Emil Forrer, who was a great authority on Hittite. So Forrer came to Hopkins and we took Hittite. It was ridiculous. Albright knew all these languages—he was amazing. He was a genius, and we were just simple human beings. He was a fantastic teacher.

In 1934 Albright invited Nelson Glueck to come and give a talk to the students. Glueck had just returned from his survey of Transjordan. If you ask me when the light, or the fire, of archaeology was lit, I think it was when Glueck came and gave a lecture on his [archaeological] survey in Transjordan. Glueck was so enthusiastic. He shared his own being with the students. When Glueck spoke about his explorations in Jordan, I decided that's what I wanted to do. There is poetic justice in the fact that 40 years later I was appointed director (at Hebrew Union College in Jerusalem) of the school named after him—the Nelson Glueck School of Biblical Archaeology.

Later, after I had gotten my Ph.D. and was living at the American School [of Oriental Research, in Jerusalem], I joined him on a trip to Tell el-Kheleifeh [near the Gulf of Eilat]. He thought it

…when I decided to go back to Palestine…her father said

THE FORMER RUTH FRANKEL and Biran after their wedding, April 6, 1936. The pair met while he was attending Johns Hopkins University in Baltimore, and Ruth followed Avraham to Palestine shortly after he returned there. She arrived on the eve of Passover; according to Jewish custom, no weddings can occur for more than a month after the onset of Passover. The pair desperately sought a rabbi who could officiate immediately. With the aid of Avraham's uncle, they were able to locate a rabbi, but he assumed that the pair wanted only a marriage of convenience to allow Ruth to stay in the country. After more than 63 years, the union is likely the longest-lasting marriage the rabbi ever performed.

AVRAHAM BIRAN

was Ezion-Geber, the seaport of King Solomon. I went with him as a driver more than anything else. That's when I learned to sleep standing up. We got to Kerak, a beautiful Crusader castle, where the Arab Legion was stationed. Glueck knew all the commanders from the days he did the survey of Transjordan. So they invited us to stay there, but there were no beds. So we stood—and that's how we fell asleep.

You stood all night?

Yes. The next day we went to Tell el-Kheleifeh, did a quick survey and established that there was pottery there from the Iron Age. So Glueck decided that he would excavate it.*

Were you a good student?

When I graduated, Albright made me a Phi Beta Kappa. I don't know whether

*The location of Ezion-Geber remains a matter of dispute. See Gary Pratico, "Where Is Ezion-Geber?" **BAR**, September/October 1986; Alexander Flinder, "Is This Solomon's Seaport?" **BAR**, July/August 1989.

that indicated I was a good student or not. I would say I was a good student because at Hopkins I did an M.A. in three years and the following year I got a Ph.D. I was Albright's first Ph.D.

But I wanted to go back to Palestine. It's something very strange, the attach-

however, you automatically could live here. A lot of Jewish girls came looking for boys to marry so they could stay in the country. My brother, for example, married such a girl. It was a fictitious marriage. They hardly knew each other. The rabbi thought that was the kind of

"Well, that's good riddance of him!"

ment I have to this country. Romantic, roots—I don't know.

Had you met Ruth at that time?

Yes. I dated her in Baltimore. I was a young man, fairly attractive. She was a piano teacher; she graduated from Peabody Conservatory. We started going together. But when I decided to go back to Palestine—Ruth is fond of telling the story—her father said, "Well, that's good riddance of him!" But then I wrote her to come to Palestine to get married. In those days, of course, you came by boat. She came to shore with a big trunk like people did in 1936.

She arrived at Haifa on Erev Pesach [the day before Passover]. And if you don't get married by Pesach, you can't get married till Lag b'Omer, 33 days later. Her family would go crazy if this happened. I asked my uncle, who was the district officer of Haifa, to arrange with the rabbi for a wedding right away. In those days Jewish immigration was restricted. If you married a Palestinian,

marriage I wanted, one of those fictitious marriages. Only when my uncle insisted—"No, look, this is a genuine marriage. You must marry her"—was a wedding arranged on Erev Pesach.

Was her family at her wedding?

No, of course not. They were in Baltimore.

Were they in favor, or were they opposed to the marriage?

They had no choice; she decided to come here and get married. What could they do?

It must have been some love affair.

Yes. It stuck to this day. In 1996 we celebrated our 60th wedding anniversary.

Tell me about your first dig.

One day when I was living at the American School, Albright said to me, "You know, there is a big argument about the identification of the Arab village of Anata [just north of Jerusalem]. Was it the birthplace of the prophet Jeremiah? Was it Biblical Anathoth?" Now, everybody had accepted

Sturman and the Sheiks

Chaim Sturman (far right), the leader of the Jewish settlements in British Mandate-era Palestine, accompanied the Birans (center) on a visit to the sheikhs of the Zenati tribe. Biran had been recently appointed by the British administration as district officer for the Beth-Shean Valley. Sturman had been born in the Ukraine in 1891 and was active in the Haganah (the military force that evolved into the Israeli army after the Jewish state declared its independence in 1948). In 1938, shortly after this photo was taken, Sturman was killed when the car he was riding in, driven by Biran, hit a land mine. He is commemorated today by Beth Sturman (Sturman House), a cultural center and museum at Kibbutz Ein Harod, which he helped found. As fate would have it, Sturman's son, Moshe, fell in Israel's War of Independence, and his grandson, also named Chaim, died in a commando action near the Suez Canal in 1969.

Wingate

Charles Orde Wingate (1903-1944), a British Army officer, served in Palestine during the 1936-1939 riots. Wingate's passionate support for the movement for a Jewish state in Palestine earned him the nickname *ha-Yedid* (the Friend) from Zionist leaders. In 1936 he played a formidable role in fighting Arab attacks on the Iraq-Haifa pipeline. Working with the Haganah, the Jewish military force, Wingate established the Special Night Squads, whose aim was to prevent and counter Arab attacks. Wingate's military genius later influenced the Israeli army. Institutions and public areas throughout Israel bear his name—in particular, Jerusalem's Wingate Square. He died in a plane crash in Burma in 1944.

CORBIS

that Anata, which is obviously the Arab pronunciation of Anathoth, is the same word. It has the same consonants. But Albrecht Alt, the great German scholar, conducted a survey at Anata and did not find any pottery from the time of Jeremiah [seventh to sixth century B.C.]. Alt suggested that the hill opposite Anata, called in Arabic Ras el-Kharrubeh (the Top of the Carob Tree, or St. John's Bread), should be identified with Anathoth because there he found pottery from the days of Jeremiah. So Albright said to me, "Why don't you go there and do a little excavation? It's a wonderful opportunity. Try your hand." So I organized a few workers and began an excavation.

Did you have any instruction in methodology, in how to dig?

I had a foreman who knew how to run the thing, and that's how you learn. I came

Anyway, Albright said to me, "Write an article." I was delighted—a fresh, new Ph.D. I wrote an article saying Ras el-Kharrubeh is not Anathoth. Albright was editor of the *Bulletin* of the American School (*BASOR*), and he said, "I'll publish it." In due course *BASOR* arrived, I turned the page, and yes, there was the identification, A. Bergman (my name at the time). I read the article. It contained everything I said. Then I turned the page: There was an article by Albright proving I'm wrong! That was typical of the man. Give the student an opportunity—right or wrong.

There's a footnote to that whole story. A few years ago, the archaeological officer in charge of Judea and Samaria came to me and said that the Arabs are building houses on Ras el-Kharrubeh and we have to do what we call an emergency dig. "Now, you excavated that way back

Two of the three people in the back of the

back and told Albright that it's true, there is pottery from the days of Jeremiah at Ras el-Kharrubeh, but according to the references in the Bible, Anathoth was already a town in the days of Solomon and David [tenth century B.C.]. It was the birthplace of two of David's military leaders [2 Samuel 23:27; 1 Chronicles 11:28, 12:3]. And I did not find any pottery from that time, so I don't think that Ras el-Kharrubeh is Anathoth.

How did you know how to date pottery?

Clarence Fisher, who excavated Samaria, worked in the basement of the American School. He was a professor of archaeology. He knew ceramic typology. And Albright did too. So I brought the pottery and showed it to them. We spread it out, and they identified [dated] the pottery.

You weren't an expert then?

Of course not. I'd just begun. That's how you begin to learn.

You had never participated in an excavation?

Not that I remember.

And you were directing the excavation?

Look, this was only a small excavation.

in 1936; would you like to go back?" I said I'd be delighted. So we organized an expedition to Ras el-Kharrubeh. This time it was a full-fledged expedition, with student workers and a supervisor in charge of each area and so forth and so on. And I still came to the same conclusion: Although there is pottery from the end of the Iron Age II [the time of Jeremiah], there isn't from the beginning. The question of Anathoth is still unsolved. I heard some time ago that in a survey done by the archaeological officer of the village of Anata, he did find early Iron Age II pottery. So maybe Anata is Anathoth, after all.

Another aspect of Albright's character: When he was director of the school, he was, of course, very friendly with Père [Louis-Hugues] Vincent [of the École Biblique et Archéologique Française in Jerusalem]. Vincent was the acknowledged leader of the archaeological community of Jerusalem. Ruth Albright [Albright's wife] came under his influence, and she became a Catholic. I remember asking Albright one day, "What are the children?" Albright gave me a look—I can still see the expression on his face—and said, "Catholic, of course, like their mother." He was a Methodist, the son of

THE SHATTERED REMAINS of a car tell of total devastation in the rear of the vehicle, but of much less damage to the front—to driver Avraham Biran's great fortune. The car's rear wheels had hit a land mine, killing Chaim Sturman and Aharon Etkin, leaders of the Jewish settlement movement in Palestine, and David Mossenson, a veterinary officer in the British administration; miraculously, Biran emerged unscratched. The mine had been placed by an Arab gang that violently opposed the growing Jewish presence in Palestine.

ar were dead. There was really no reason for me to be alive.

a minister, but he accepted the way things were. He was just saying that if the mother is Catholic she teaches them, she educates them. It's only natural. I think one of his sons became a priest.

All the Israeli archaeologists worked with Albright at Tell Beit Mirsim. [Benjamin] Mazar worked there. I think [E.L.] Sukenik worked there. [Shmuel] Yeivin worked there. When they established an archaeology department at the Hebrew University, Yeivin was a candidate for appointment as professor, but Albright suggested Sukenik. He felt Sukenik would do a better job. So everybody went for Sukenik. Albright organized the Palestine Oriental Society and for ten years edited the *Journal of the Palestine Oriental Society*. Albright was the great one.

Years later, in 1937, when I was offered a job with the Palestine government, I told Albright about the offer. It was a good job in those days—it paid 29 pounds a month—but it would take me away from archaeology. Albright said to me, "Well, if you want to be an archaeologist, you have to do one of two things. Either marry a rich widow, like Professor Yahuda did, or marry a detective writer, like Max Mallowan did." He married Agatha Christie. "Well," Albright said,

"You're already married; you better take the job." I became the district officer for the Valley of Beth-Shean. The country was divided into districts. The British adopted the division of the country from the Turks. The Turks had these districts, and there was a *kaimakam* (a Turkish word meaning "governor"). The *kaimakam* in the days of the Turkish Empire was very powerful. There was a *kaimakam* in Nazareth, there was a *kaimakam* in Jerusalem, there was a *kaimakam* in Jaffa. The British adopted this system and appointed a district commissioner in each district. After the Arab riots in 1936, the Jewish settlements didn't want to go to the district officers in the Arab towns to conduct their business, and they demanded Jewish district officers in Jewish areas. For the Emeq [the Valley], I was offered the job.

How did you happen to be offered that job?

You know, life is made up of accidents. At the teacher's training college, I shared the bench with a fellow named Reuven Zaslany (later Shiloah). He was the son of a rabbi who lived in Jerusalem's Bukharan Quarter. Reuven and I got to be friendly. When I went to study in America, he was sent by the Jewish

Agency to Iraq to teach Hebrew to the Jewish kids in Baghdad. When he came back, he became head of intelligence. Because he was doing intelligence work, the Jewish Agency asked him to take care of the problem of the Jewish settlements wanting Jewish district officers. So he came to me and said, "Look, I have an idea. Why don't you accept the job of district officer?" I said, "Me? I'm an archaeologist." I had just published my dissertation in the *Journal of the Palestine Oriental Society*. But he said, "You know, it's not just any job. You'd be going to the Emeq." In Hebrew, *emeq* means just "valley." But then it had a great symbolic significance. It was the Emeq Jezreel, the Jezreel Valley. The Emeq represented all the magnificence of the new Jewish settlements in Israel. To work in the Emeq is like for you to be in Washington in Congress. The Jewish settlements in the Emeq were the workshop of the new Israel. Finally, I took the job.

When you accepted that job, you were effectively leaving archaeology, weren't you?

Well, I didn't know. Some people know from childhood what they're going to do. I didn't. If I hadn't gone to the Reali ... Look, as a farmer's son I could have gone to Mikveh Israel Agricultural School near Tel Aviv, which was founded by Baron Rothschild to teach young Jews to be good farmers. My uncles thought this was a wonderful opportunity. Here was a poor orphan boy: Go—and I almost went. My mother, who felt that her children should be educated, refused. She said she'd take us to the Reali. Whether that killed her or not, I don't know. She was a widow with three small children. We lived in one room in downtown Haifa, where the marketplace is. One cannot imagine today conditions as they were then. If I had gone to Mikveh Israel, maybe today I would be a famous agricultural officer.

The only thing I did on my own was go to America. I wasn't quite sure what I wanted to do. If I hadn't met Albright, and if he hadn't offered me that scholarship, who knows? Later, if I had not been offered the job in the Emeq, who knows? I don't think I have ever in my life made an application for a job.

Tell me about your work in the Emeq.

The Jewish settlements, whenever they had any demands, would come to me, and I would pass them on to the British authorities. The British high commissioner, Arthur Wauchope, used to come to visit. He was very interested in agriculture. We'd be driving around, and once he stopped the car and asked, "What is this field?" I said it was barley, or whatever it was. He said, "Good, that's what my agriculture inspector said to me, too." He was testing to see how his people were doing.

When there were political issues, the settlements would send in a delegation to see me. At that time, we had opened an office in Afula. That separated the [Jewish] settlements from the Arab villages.

One day, sometime in September of 1938, people

from the Jewish National Fund came to have a look at the settlements, and I decided to go with them. We were a convoy of cars with supernumerary [additional British] police following us in a tender [an open truck with benches in the back]. By then the British had appointed military units to guard the settlements. They also guarded the petroleum line from Iraq to Haifa, which ran through the Emeq. Arab gangs had attacked the pipeline and burned it. That's when Orde Wingate came. He was a British officer sent to protect the pipeline, and he decided that the way to protect it was by anticipating the attacks of the gangs rather than waiting until they attacked. He would look for the gangs before they were able to attack. He trained the Jews in night fighting. The whole principle changed at that time. Until then the settlements were simply stockades with a watchtower. After Wingate, it was for attack instead of only defense.

Anyway, our convoy decided to have a look at the settlement of Maoz. In my car was Chaim Sturman, the recognized head of the settlements; the chairman of the settlements committee, Aharon Etkin; and my friend David Mossenson, a veterinary officer employed by the Palestine administration; and, in the front seat, a British police-

man, who was acting as my guard. We went to Maoz and saw what they were doing, and we discussed their plans and so forth. Then we went to look at the site of what eventually became Kfar Rupin. From there we could see Tirat Zvi, which was a religious settlement that a few days earlier had repulsed a very severe attack by the gangs. So we wanted to see it. But we couldn't get through because the area was muddy and full of swamps. So we decided to go back to Beth-Shean and from Beth-Shean we would follow the road that goes to Jericho, and from there you turn left to Tirat Zvi. At Beth-Shean the tender of the supernumerary police that had accompanied us left us to go with a car from the Jewish National Fund that was going back to Jerusalem; the tender was to guard them to Beth Alpha; from Beth Alpha the road was fairly safe, and the police tender could come back and accompany us. We would wait for them to come back, and then it would go with us down to Tirat Zvi. It was a very hot day, about 1:30 in the afternoon in September, and Chaim Sturman said, "Eh, let's go. Why wait for the tender?" So we said okay. We got into the car. I was driving, with the policeman next to me, and Sturman, Etkin and Mossenson were in the back seat. As we drove south past an experimental agricultural station, suddenly, as we passed the corner, I saw a lot of dust in front of us. I didn't realize what it was. I was still holding the wheel. I stopped and opened the door and started walking; then I saw all three people from the back seat on the ground in front of me. It was a bomb that had gone off. Luckily for me, it was activated by the rear wheels rather than the front wheels. If it had been the front wheels, I would have been killed. The policeman came out with me, and we were going toward the three people when suddenly shots were fired at us. The policeman had a gun and I had a gun, a small revolver, but it was very hot and I had

LEWIS ANDREWS, a district governor in Palestine, cuts a dashing figure in Arab headdress, à la Lawrence of Arabia. Biran remembers Andrews as a wonderful person who was very friendly to the Jewish settlements in Palestine. Andrews, too, was a victim of the violence in the region: He was killed in an attack on a Sunday morning as he was going to church in Nazareth.

AVRAHAM BIRAN

DAVID RUBINGER/JERUSALEM POST/COURTESY OF AVRAHAM BIRAN

SERVING AS DIRECTOR of the Israel Department of Antiquities and Museums (today the Israel Antiquities Authority), Biran (center) leads a group of dignitaries on a 1962 visit to the just-discovered Cave of Letters, a site in the Judean wilderness that yielded a trove of documents and personal items belonging to a group of Jews hiding from the Romans during the Second Jewish Revolt (132-135 B.C.). At far left is Teddy Kollek, at the time head of Israel's tourism office and soon to become Jerusalem's long-serving mayor (1965-1993); in the light jacket is Benjamin Mazar, one of Israel's most distinguished archaeologists, who was later to excavate the area around the Temple Mount; in the background, between Mazar and Biran, is Joseph Aviram, then the director of Hebrew University's Institute of Archaeology and today the longtime head of the Israel Exploration Society; at far right is General Avraham Yoffe.

taken it out and left it on the seat beside me. But the policeman had his rifle with him, and he began shooting at the gang, who continued to shoot at us. We ran to the field by the road. Very interesting what you think when you have shots fired at you. I had recently read a book about a newspaperman who was on a plane flying from India to Egypt, and the plane suddenly started to go down. He wrote that he saw sharks in the water and said to himself, "Well, I'm going to die. What am I thinking of?" As we were running around the boulders and the irrigation ditches, dodging the bullets—all of this must have been

seconds, of course—I suddenly remembered that book and I said to myself, "Well, I'm going to die. What am I thinking of?" Then I said to myself, "Well, I think I'm not going to die." We kept on going and I stumbled and the policeman was hit by a bullet that went through his face. He fell down. All of this must have taken only seconds, but it seemed like an eternity. I went to him. Suddenly I saw, from a distance, the supernumerary police tender arriving. They had come back. We didn't see the tender coming, but the Arab gang saw it and ran away.

Two of the three people in the back seat were already dead. Chaim Sturman was still alive and moaning, so I thought maybe we could get him back and save him. We put the three of them on the tender and drove back to Beth-Shean. There was a British police force in Beth-Shean, but they were barricaded in. We knocked on the door, we yelled at them, we told them there was a gang down there. They finally opened the door. We told them that we were taking the wounded man to a doctor at a settlement near Beth-Shean. But by the time we got there, it was too late: Sturman died. He couldn't be saved.

I telephoned Ruth and told her to go and see Varda Mossenson, with whom we were friendly. They also lived in Afula.

Ruth said, "What happened?" I said, "A land mine, he's dead." "Oh, my God." Then after a second, she said, "How are you?" I was talking to her, so I must have been in a condition where I could speak to her. I did not have even a scratch. There was really no reason for me to be alive. Three people were dead. The back of the car was blown up. Perhaps it's compensation because my parents died very young. Today in Kibbutz Ein Harod, where Sturman lived, there is the Sturman House—Beth Sturman—a center for culture and a museum. The policeman who had sat next to me was hospitalized and recovered.

Over time, the various district governors changed. An Australian named Lewis Andrews, a wonderful man, very friendly to the [Jewish] settlements, was killed by the gangs on a Sunday morning as he was going to church in Nazareth.

A man named J.H.H. Pollock was governor of the Galilee district. In 1945 he was transferred to Jerusalem. So he said to me, "How about coming with me to Jerusalem and becoming a district officer in Jerusalem?" I was a little bit hesitant. You see, in the Emeq, I was king.

I have a story for you about being king. The Hebrew term for district officer is *katzin mechoz*. But the people called us *moshel*, "governor." One day Dr. [Shlomo

Dov] Goitein, one of my teachers at the Reali, came to visit. He later became very famous for his work on the Cairo Genizah.* When he came to Afula, he asked for the house of the *katzin ha-mechoz*, the district officer. Nobody knew. He asked people. Nobody knew. Finally, he said Avraham Bergman. They said, "Ah, *ha-moshel*! You want the governor! That's where he lives."

So there I was, king in a small pond. Should I go to Jerusalem, with all the problems of Jerusalem? But Ruth said, "Why don't we try it?" So I did. I had been in the Emeq from 1937 to 1945. So I came with Pollock to Jerusalem.

In 1946 or 1947, the British Council arranged a course for officials from different countries around the world to come to England to study local government. The British government in Palestine decided to send two district officers for this training. At that time, people were already talking about the British leaving the country. I remember talking to Pollock and saying, "I don't understand. You say you are going to leave Palestine, and

---

*The Cairo Genizah is a trove of about 140,000 medieval manuscripts recovered from a Cairo synagogue. See S.D. Goitein, *A Mediterranean Society* (Berkeley, CA: Univ. of California Press, 1967).

you want to send us for a course to England." He replied, "That's how we operate in the British Empire. We go on as if nothing changed." That's a lesson I learned, and I tried to teach it to others: You carry on with your work no matter what. Anyway, I and an Arab colleague from Tulkarm, another district officer, were chosen to go to this course. When we came back, all of my colleagues here said, "Don't you dare write a bad report [about the value of the course]. We all want to have a chance to go afterwards!"

You spent eight years in the Emeq. Did you have anything to do with archaeology in those years?

Together with Ruth Amiran [then Ruth Bransteter], we did an archaeological survey of the Beth-Shean Valley, which we published in Hebrew. I remained very close to the Israel Exploration Society. There was a great deal of interest in the land and its ancient history. [Benjamin] Mazar [then Maisler], [Nahman] Avigad and Michael Avi-Yonah all used to come to the Emeq and lecture on the work they were doing—at Beth Yerah, and at Beth Alpha. We would visit the sites.

When I came to Jerusalem, there was no time for that, just for administration.

ISRAELI SOLDIERS CAPTURE the Rockefeller Museum in the battle for Jerusalem during the Six-Day War in June 1967. During the height of the fighting, Biran, Joseph Aviram and archaeologist Nahman Avigad approached the military commander and asked for permission to enter the museum to secure its holdings. Biran saw to it that an exhibit of gold jewelry on display at the time was locked away. He also secured the inscriptions from Deir Alla, a site in Jordan, and later returned them to the Dutch team that was deciphering them; today the inscriptions are in Amman, Jordan. But the most famous prize at the Rockefeller was the collection of Dead Sea Scrolls. Together with Yigael Yadin, Biran made the controversial decision to leave the publication rights with the team that had been appointed under Jordanian auspices. That team later came under withering criticism for its glacially slow pace of publication.

In 1947 Israel accepted the United Nations resolution partitioning Palestine and internationalizing Jerusalem. Today, of course, to revive that resolution is silly. But at that time we accepted the fact that Jerusalem would be internationalized. Dov Yosef, a lawyer from Jerusalem and a member of the Jewish Agency, was appointed military governor because under international law even west Jerusalem was occupied territory. He asked me to be his deputy because I had been district officer and knew the administration. It was only later—in 1949—that the government of Israel decided to make Jerusalem its capital. We moved various ministries to Jerusalem then, including the Ministry of the Interior, and Dov Yosef was appointed to a cabinet ministry. He was actually the Minister of Austerity. He was in charge of the allocations of food and water for the city. Everything was in a terrible state. Then the Ministry of the Interior decided to appoint district commissioners, just like the old days, but they didn't like the term *moshel*. The *Jerusalem Post* didn't like the translation of *ha-memu-neh al ha-mechoz* as "district commissioner." They preferred to translate it "district representative." That's how I became the first district representative of Jerusalem. But people who remembered the old days when the district commissioner was called *moshel* still used that term. So at least colloquially I was the governor of Jerusalem.

At the time my name was still Bergman, and I wanted to change it to a Hebrew name. I tried several possibilities. For a time, I called myself Ben Aharon, the son of Aharon. My father's name was Aharon. Because Berg means mountain, I used the Aramaic word for mountain, *tura*, but in Aramaic, if you change the *tet* to *tav*, it means an ox. I decided not to take that name.

One day Dr. Goitein, my old teacher, telephoned me and said, "I have a name for you." I said, "What?" He said "Biran." I said, "Why?" He said, "First of all, it has a *B* as in Bergman. Secondly, Biran comes from the word *birah*, "capital." Jerusalem has been declared the capital, and you are the governor of the capital. Besides that, the kings of Judah built fortifications around Jerusalem, and in the Hebrew Bible the word is *biraniot* [2 Chronicles 17:12, 27:4]. You are trying to build Jerusalem so it will be safe. So why not Biran?" So the next morning I paid 25 piastres, or whatever it was, and changed my name officially to Biran.

A lot of people were changing their names at that time.

Yes, because [David] Ben Gurion [Israel's first prime minister] wanted Hebrew names. At that time the Negev was full of Arab names. The army had captured the Negev, but it was very difficult for the Israeli soldiers to follow or remember these names. So Ben Gurion appointed a names committee for the Negev, and he appointed me chairman. We decided to change the names of the mountains and the wadis [dry riverbeds] to give them a historical connotation whenever possible. In the Bible lots of names are mentioned. Way back in the 1920s, the Jewish Settlement Fund had a similar committee to name new settlements. The government decided to join the two committees and called it the Government Names Committee. In 1951 I was appointed chairman of the larger committee. I'm still the chairman of that committee.

When you chose a Biblical name for a site, how sure were you that the name really fit?

We used only names of which we were sure. Take Beth-Shean. When the Romans conquered Beth-Shean, they called it Scythopolis. Throughout the Byzantine period it was called Scythopolis. When the Arabs conquered the country, it became Beisan. Beisan is obviously Beth-Shean. So there was no difficulty in identifying it. There are many such names that can easily be traced.

The Arabs had a Bedouin camp called Ara'ir. Nelson Glueck saw it when he did his survey of the Negev. Obviously,

AVRAHAM BIRAN/HEBREW UNION COLLEGE–JEWISH INSTITUTE OF RELIGION

Thirty-four Years and Counting...

Lush greenery surrounds the site of Tel Dan, located in Israel's far north near the source of the Jordan River and the foothills of Mount Hermon. Biran began excavations at the site in 1966—and has not stopped since. The dig is the longest-running excavation in Israel and has yielded an impressive array of Israelite cultic sites and ritual artifacts.

One of Biran's most spectacular finds at Dan is the inscribed stone slab, discovered in three chunks, shown above. Biran dates it to the mid-ninth century B.C.; he and epigrapher Joseph Naveh believe the inscription contains a boast by the king of Damascus, who claims to have defeated the king of the northern kingdom of Israel and the king of "the house of David." The overwhelming majority of scholars agree with this reading, which would be the first historical reference outside the Bible to a Davidic dynasty and, by inference, to King David.

Ara'ir in Arabic is Aroer in Hebrew, the city mentioned in the Bible. After his victory over the Amalekites, David sends the booty to the elders of Judah; among them were the elders of Aroer [1 Samuel 30:26-28].

Or take Dan, where I have dug for 33 years. Over 160 years ago Edward Robinson—an American—identified Tell el-Qadi as ancient Dan because in Arabic Tell el-Qadi means the "Mound of the Judge," and Dan in Hebrew means "judge." This has been fairly well accepted, but one young scholar who worked with us at Dan said it could not be Dan. It is true that the identification of a site, applying historical evidence, is often very doubtful. But in our case, if we had any doubts about the identification

of Tell el-Qadi as Tel Dan, they were dispelled when we found a bilingual inscription in Greek and Aramaic, which says, "To the God who is in Dan." That definitely settles the argument.

What about a place like Philistine Gath. You're not at all sure, are you, of that identification?

To this day, nobody knows Gath's identity.

You gave a settlement that name.

Yes, a town, because it's somewhere in the neighborhood. It has to be.

When we came to name the new town of Arad, we had a problem. Yohanan Aharoni and Ruth Amiran were excavating Arad—it includes a beautiful ancient Israelite fortress and an Early Bronze Age town.* The new town was 8 kilometers away from the ancient site. Aharoni suggested we call the new town Arad. I said to him, "Look, it's five miles away." "So," he said to me, "You know that names travel." I said, "But not such a distance!" He said, "Well, this is the

*See Ze'ev Herzog, Miriam Aharoni and Anson F. Rainey, "Arad—An Ancient Israelite Fortress with a Temple of Yahweh," **BAR,** March/April 1987; Ruth Amiran, Rolf Goethert and Ornit Olan, "The Well of Arad," **BAR,** March/April 1987.

Negev, and in the Negev names travel further away than in the hills." So we named the new town Arad.

A book has now been published by the Government Names Committee giving all of the names that were given since the State of Israel was established.

How long were you governor of Jerusalem?

That went on until 1955. By 1955 the Foreign Ministry had moved to Jerusalem. I was still a member of the armistice commission established after the War of Independence. The relationship between Israel and Jordan had stabilized. We had done a lot of work in Jerusalem—all the new development, all the new neighborhoods. I didn't think of moving to anything else, but the office of the Foreign Ministry came to me and said, "Look, we have a problem. The American administration is now Republican"—Eisenhower was president—"we would like to appoint you consul general in Los Angeles for the 11 western states so you can go and meet people and try to make friends." It was an interesting challenge. I thought I had exhausted my possibilities as governor of Jerusalem,

THE PRESIDENT OF ISRAEL, Ephraim Katzir (center), and Hebrew Union College president Alfred Gottschalk (far right) view the high place at Dan during a visit in the mid-1970s. Between them is Vassilios Tzaferis, Biran's longtime colleague.

The Bible records that after the death of Solomon, Jeroboam established a breakaway kingdom in the north of Israel. He built shrines at Bethel and at Dan to keep worshipers from Jerusalem; at each shrine, he erected a golden calf. Although Biran has yet to find the calf, he believes that the idol stood at this high place.

so I said, "Fine." But I said, "I have two grown children. Ronny [Aharon], my oldest son, will be going to the army in two years. I don't want to be in America when he goes to the army. I don't want to stay there longer than two years." They said, "OK." So we went to Los Angeles, and we developed the consulate there.

The first man I met was Mendel Silberberg, a lawyer in Los Angeles. He was head of a very important law firm and was a great friend of Nixon's. That's how I began my contacts with the Republicans. Then I went to San Francisco and met Walter and Elise Haas. Walter was a friend of Senator Knowland. Through him I met Senator Knowland.

All Work and Some Play

After you've been digging for 34 years, you're entitled to a little fun. The staff and students from the Tel Dan excavation enjoy the refreshing waterfall at nearby Banias (Caesarea Philippi). Many of them were not even born when Avraham Biran began excavating the site.

Years later, when I was head of the Department of Antiquities and we wanted to excavate at Tel Dan, I went back to Walter Haas and said to him, "I need some funds for the excavation." The Haas family are actually the ones who started me on the excavation of Tel Dan. Walter Haas has been dead many years, but to this day their descendants still support the dig at Tel Dan.

After 33 years?

Yes, a remarkable thing. Peter and Mimi Haas visited our excavations at Dan and Aroer as well as our museum on campus. Richard and Rhoda Goldman came to Dan and brought their children. So I put them to work on the dig. Their children, now grown, are dear friends. Moreover, they bring their children and are coming to work this summer at the dig.

So that's three generations?

Actually, four generations if you count Walter and Elise Haas.

Anyway, when my two years in Los Angeles were up, I said, "It's time to go back." That was 1957, when following the Russian invasion of Hungary there was a lot of turmoil. The government said to me, "All right, we promised you two years but this is a very new situation. Stay another year." So we stayed in Los Angeles until 1958.

When I came back, I became director of armistice affairs in the Foreign Ministry.

Whenever you

I negotiated with the Jordanians, with the United Nations.

In 1961 [Shmuel] Yeivin, who was head of the Department of Antiquities, resigned to start an archaeology department at Tel Aviv University. When Yeivin went down to head the Department of Archaeology, Mazar, Avi-Yonah, Avigad and others came to me and said, "Why don't you take over [the Department of Antiquities]?" I said, "It will be really difficult. It has been many years since I was actively engaged [in archaeology]." I remember them saying to me,

THE CANAANITE GATEWAY. Biran and assistant Hanni Hirsch view Dan's massive mudbrick gate, which was discovered in 1979 and dates to about 1800 B.C. The arch spans 8 feet; the entire structure—the central gateway and flanking towers—measures 50 feet across and is preserved to a height of 20 feet. The gateway owes its preservation to the fact that the Canaanites buried it under a huge defensive rampart that they later built around the city. But Biran and his team had to contend with the fear that if they cleared the gateway, it would collapse. They opted to expose only one half of the structure and to keep the archway filled in.

AVRAHAM BIRAN/HEBREW UNION COLLEGE—JEWISH INSTITUTE OF RELIGION

"Precisely what we need—we want somebody fresh."

I remember speaking to Albright on a trip to America. I told him, "They are offering me this job. What do you think?" Albright looked at me and said, "You know, with your Arabic and your Hebrew and your background, you'll do a good job." So I said, "Fine." I took the job. I became the director of the Department of Antiquities and Museums. That was really a wonderful opportunity.

The highlight was, of course, the Six-Day War in 1967. In May of that year, I was already digging at Tel Dan. Toward the beginning of June, suddenly all my young assistants were disappearing. They were being called to the army. The war started on Monday, June 5. By the previous Friday, I had decided this was crazy: Everybody's joining the war. What am I doing up here? So we went

dig you destroy. All excavation is destruction.

to Jerusalem and started helping the Israel Museum move all of the objects down to the cellar for protection. The building itself was not hit during the war, but a shell fired by the Jordanian army fell into the museum compound.

The night of the first day of the war, I got a telephone call from Yigael Yadin's wife, Carmela. He had been called back into service as adviser to [Prime Minister Levi] Eshkol. Carmela said that Yigael had just called from Tel Aviv: "The army is going into the Rockefeller [Museum]. Go down and see if you can

find the Dead Sea Scrolls." So [Nahman] Avigad and [Joseph] Aviram of the Israel Exploration Society and I went down at 7:30 the next morning to the headquarters of the unit that was engaged in the battle of Jerusalem, to [Commander] Motta [Mordechai] Gur, and I said to him, "Motta, we want to go to the Rockefeller." He gave us a look—these crazy guys. He was trying to capture the Old City, to conquer the Rockefeller. The Arab Legion was on the walls of the Old City shooting into the Rockefeller. This bunch of crazy guys wants to go to the

Rockefeller? That was the 6th of June. So I said to him, "Okay, we'll go away, now. We'll come back in another few hours. Around 10:30 the three of us came back. I said to him, "Motta, well, can we go to the Rockefeller?" He gives us a look and says, "All right, I'm going now. Come with me." So we got into a command car, and we drove down to the Mandelbaum Gate and one car blew up on a land mine. But we got to the Rockefeller from the back while the shooting continued from the Old City wall. It wasn't until the next day that we captured the Old City. Our soldiers were already in the Rockefeller and they were shooting back but you still couldn't go in. So I told Motta, "Look, I remember there is an entrance from the courtyard, from the back." So we started to go there. As we approached, we saw a Jordanian officer who was my opposite number in the armistice agreement meetings; he was hurt. He had an assistant with him, so I told his assistant, "Carry him to the Arab Legion headquarters." Then we went in through the back door and moved along the corridors, where the soldiers were sitting who had been fighting and battling through the night. They were exhausted.

Long before, I had organized something called "trustees of antiquities" in every village and town. These people became the ears and eyes of the Department of Antiquities. They would notify us when there was any encroachment on an antiquity site. We would have regular meetings and give them lectures. As we were walking through the corridors of the Rockefeller hoping to find the Dead Sea Scrolls, a soldier, tired and sleepy—I can still see him—opened his eyes. He looked at me and yelled, "Hey, that's the director of the Department of Antiquities! Fellows, we're going to have a conducted tour of the museum!" He was one of our trustees of antiquities from one of the villages.

The Jordanians had an exhibit of gold jewelry at that time. So the first thing I did was to get hold of the Arab guard and ask him, "Where's the key?" He had the key and I said, "Lock the door [of the room where the gold was displayed]."

Then I said, "Where are your inscriptions?" He took us to another door. We opened it, and there were all of the inscriptions from the Dutch expedition at Deir Alla, the inscriptions that mention the prophet Baalam [Numbers 22-24]. So we locked that door. A few months later, a delegation from Holland came to see me: They had a request from the Queen of Holland. "By all means, what can I do for you?" They wanted us to give them the Deir Alla inscriptions. I remember telling them, "What do you think, that we are barbarians, that we would take the Deir Alla inscriptions that you excavated and publish them ourselves? We'll give them back to you." At that time, nobody knew what the inscriptions contained. Deir Alla is in Jordan, so the Deir Alla inscriptions are now in Amman.

Anyway, after we secured the Deir Alla inscriptions, we started looking for the Dead Sea Scrolls, but we didn't find them. When the battle of the Old City was completed, we went back to the Rockefeller and found a passageway from the first floor down to the cellar, to the underground storerooms, and there we found the scrolls. One of the Arab officials, whom I later took on to work with the Israel Department of Antiquities, told me that the Jordanian government had asked to have the Dead Sea Scrolls shipped to Amman. The staff at the Rockefeller was ready to ship them and had asked the authorities in Amman to send a tender to take them, but the tender never arrived. So they put them down in the basement. Yadin wanted to move the scrolls to the Shrine of the Book [part of the Israel Museum in West Jerusalem] and the publication of the scrolls to appear under the name of the Shrine of the Book. But they remained at the Rockefeller.

When the British built the Rockefeller Museum, they engraved the stone identification plaques on the walls in the three official languages—Hebrew, Arabic and English. The Jordanians had covered the Hebrew. We removed the covering.

[British archaeologist] Kathleen Kenyon was digging in Jerusalem at this time, wasn't she?

Yes, she had been digging in [the part of] Jerusalem [controlled by Jordan]. After the war she found herself digging in Israel. Soon after the war she and, I believe, Diana Kirkbride published a letter in the *London Times* saying that Israel had no right to Jerusalem. After all, the Arabs have been here for so long. I read it, and I was a little upset. One day I was informed that Kathleen Kenyon wanted to see me. So she came to my office. I said to her, "You are a historian, you are a scholar. What kind of a letter did you write? What do you mean saying that we have no association with Jerusalem? From David and Solomon!" She didn't answer. Then she said she would like to continue her excavation. So I said, "Fine. Write an application, and we'll give you a license." She asked for a license not for working down near the [Gihon] Spring, where she had made all her biggest discoveries, but for working near the Dung Gate, and we gave her the license. She was cold and stiff, and our relations were correct. She had never been to Israel before '67, but years later she also visited me at Tel Dan.

When did you begin digging at Tel Dan?

The year before the Six-Day War. We didn't go there because it was the site of Biblical Dan or even because that's where we thought it was. It was near the border with Syria and Lebanon, at the source of the Jordan River. The army had been digging trenches and putting up gun emplacements facing the Syrian positions. Some kibbutzniks from Kibbutz Dan, a couple of miles from the tell, came and told me that the army was destroying the tell. So we decided to do a quick little excavation to see what we could learn before either the army destroyed much of the evidence or who knows what the result of a war could be. If war broke out, we might not be able to go there. So we rushed to do what we call a rescue dig. Of course, we knew from the Bible that Jeroboam had set up the golden calf at Dan [1 Kings 12:28-30]. We thought it might be interesting to see if we could find the locality where the golden calf would have been set. Could we find the sanctuary or the high place where the cult rituals took place?

Did you think you might be able to find the golden calf itself?

Deep in your heart, you always think, "Wouldn't it be wonderful to find the golden calf."

We went to the northern edge of the tell, where the springs are. We wanted to work there, but the army wouldn't let us because this faced the Syrian positions. The army said that if we started working there and bringing in a lot of people, it might become a cause for war. So we said to the army, "So where can we dig?" They said on the southern slope. Okay, so we went to the southern slope. But it is about 200 yards long—where to begin? We saw two huge rocks—built stones—jutting out of the slope. So we said if we can cut a trench between these two blocks of stones, maybe we'll learn something without doing any damage. It happened that it was a very fortunate choice because we discovered over the years that these stones were part of the gate from the Israelite period.

Did you make that choice based on your expertise as an archaeologist? Did you have some experience that told you to do that? Or was it simply common sense? Or luck?

Well, I think common sense is a very important element in excavating. Obviously these built stones represented some construction. To remove them would be against everything that you've been taught. So we chose an area that was between them.

Whenever you dig, you destroy. All excavation is a destruction. We cut a trench through the southern slope to see whether we could learn something about the construction of the ramparts that protected the city. We could have started at the bottom, at the foot of the rampart. Had we done that, we might have discovered in 1966 the inscription that we found in 1993 that mentions the "House of David." Who knows? It's all chance, whatever you do. The trench we cut was a fortunate one because when we reached the bottom, we found a stone pavement. That's all we knew at the beginning. Then we discovered that the stones we had seen jutting out of the rampart were part of a wall. Next to it was a paved area. I had no idea what this paved area was. But in subsequent years all we did was simply follow the pavement eastward to the threshold of the gate. Later we went west and found that this paved road led all the way to the top of the mound.

After the war the army said we could dig anywhere we wanted. It was only then that we undertook to excavate the area where we thought we might find the golden calf—if you like to be a little facetious. Here again, an interesting thing happened. After removing less than an inch of topsoil, we came upon a platform of beaten white earth. We wondered what it was. The army still had its headquarters in a house they built in that area. They came and said it was built by a regiment long ago; it was not an antiquity. But as we continued working, we found some Roman sherds. We realized that it was a Roman platform. The young archaeologist in charge of that area was a former Greek priest, Vassilios Tzaferis. So everyone said, "Of course, you put Vassilios to work and he finds something Roman." Then, at the edge of the platform he found a niche facing east. So everybody said, "Ah, Vassilios found a church." Churches are directed east. Eventually it turned out that this was an area that had been used as a kiln, where they burnt lime during the Muslim period. Vassilios kept on digging, and eventually he found there the remains of an Israelite sanctuary, the beginning of which was dated to the end of the tenth century [B.C.]. It seems to us that we have here the remains of the high place that Jeroboam built 3,000 years ago.

We've been digging at Dan now for 33 years. People ask me today, "When are you going to stop?" I say that it reminds me of an old Jewish story of a guy desperately fighting with a bear. His friends keep yelling at him to let go of the bear. "I want to," he says, "but the bear won't let me go."

Why do you suppose Biblical archaeologists have been so heavily criticized in recent years for being biased, for trying to prove the Bible? What's the source of the anti-Biblical archaeology movement?

It is undoubtedly connected with two things: Liberal-minded people think that Biblical archaeology supports the Fundamentalists. Take, for example, the Israeli archaeologist Emmanuel Anati, now living in Italy, who has been looking for Mt. Sinai. Professor Anati is a real authority on rock art. He did a fantastic job of explaining drawings that he found in Spain, in southern France

and also in the Negev. Professor Anati maintains that Har Karkom, a mountain in the Negev with rock drawings, is the traditional Mt. Sinai. He's sure that it is.* So people who object to Biblical archaeology say, "You are looking for Mt. Sinai. You want to establish the veracity of Moses giving the Ten Commandments to the Israelites." Archaeologists do not aim to do that.

I cannot refrain from thinking that there is also a little bit of anti-Israel or, if you like, anti-Semitism in some of the anti-Biblical archaeology people.** After all, modern Israel is reestablishing, in a way, the kingdom of David and Solomon. If there was no David and there was no Solomon, as some of them contend, there's nothing to reestablish. Look what happened to the inscription we found at Tel Dan mentioning *Beth David*, the House, or Dynasty, of David. The Hebrew consonants are clear—*bet, yod, tav, dalet, vav, dalet*. Anybody who sees this can only think that it's *Beth David*, House of David. It also clearly mentions "king of Israel"; nobody can deny this.† When [Harvard professor] Larry Stager read what the so-called Biblical minimalists were saying against the House of David inscription, he said, "It's like saying today 150 years after Lincoln, there was no Lincoln." This inscription dates to less than 150 years after David. It was written by an Aramean king who says he killed the king of Israel and killed the king of the House of David, the king of Judah. Those who deny there was a David take the consonants *dalet, vav, dalet* and say the *D* and the *V* and the *D* represent the word *dod*, "uncle" or "lover"; or even *doad*, which is a big vessel.††

In rabbinic learning there is the *pshat* and the *drash*. The *pshat* is the simple meaning of the words. The rabbis wisely say that you should always look first for the obvious, simple meaning of a word. And the obvious meaning here is David!

What Albright said bears repeating: The Bible as a divine book needs no proof. I am not out to prove that the story about Dan

*Emmanuel Anati, "Has Mt. Sinai Been Found?" **BAR**, July/August 1985; Israel Finkelstein, "Raider of the Lost Mountain—An Israeli Archaeologist Looks at the Most Recent Attempt to Locate Mt. Sinai," **BAR**, July/August 1988.

See Hershel Shanks, "The Biblical Minimalists: Expunging Ancient Israel's Past," *Bible Review*, June 1997; "Scholar Claims Palestinian History Is Suppressed in Favor of Israelites," **BAR, March/April 1996.

†"'David' Found at Dan," **BAR**, March/April 1994; David Noel Freedman and Jeffrey C. Geoghegan, "'House of David' Is There!" **BAR**, March/April 1995.

††See Philip R. Davies, "'House of David' Built on Sand," **BAR**, July/August 1994.

in the Book of Judges [about how Canaanite Laish became Israelite Dan] is correct. I simply tell you that following the rich Middle Bronze and Late Bronze Age civilization at the site identified with Dan, there is a complete change in the physical remains.

I'll give you an example where maybe I stretch a point of Biblical archaeology, and you can use that against me. We found in the Israelite level of occupation at Tel Dan very extensive remains of metalworks. We found copper slag. We found crucibles. We found the pipes that carried the air to the furnace. Archaeologically speaking, you have some kind of metalworks here. I'm intrigued by a verse in the Second Book of Chronicles in which Solomon asks the king of Tyre to send him experts to work in bronze and iron [2 Chronicles 2:7]. The king of Tyre compliments Solomon on his wisdom and says, "I'm sending you a man who is an expert." Then he says the man's mother is "from the daughters of Dan" [2 Chronicles 2:13-14]. Was the king of Tyre interested in telling Solomon that the man's mother was Jewish, that she's a member of the tribe of Dan? Why? I don't think so. Until we discovered the metalworks at Dan, the verse remained a puzzle. Now I believe that the king of Tyre was trying to show Solomon that the man really is an expert, he comes from a tradition of metalworkers. He comes from the tribe of Dan, which had already excelled in metalworks.

Why do you say that that can be used against you?

Because it's as though I'm trying to prove the veracity of the verse in the Book of Chronicles. I'm not trying to prove it. I'm simply trying to understand the significance of these three Hebrew words.

What is historical in the Bible is not for me to say. As an archaeologist, I will not enter into that. All I will say, for example, is that if there is a reference in the Bible to a city, Dan, which at an earlier time was called Laish [Judges 18], in the second millennium B.C., I have such a city. Whether Abraham came there, I don't know. Whether he existed, it's not for me to prove.

As a child I believed in a God with a white beard that sits in a big chair and guards over me. And now, at close to 90, I have no reason to doubt it. I am still able to go out and work, to sit with you and talk to you at length about Biblical archaeology, or, like yesterday, to deliver a lecture in Tel Aviv about the Canaanite city of Laish that became the Israelite city of Dan. Do you want to call it Providence? Do you want to call it fate? I don't care. I have my God who is sitting there in heaven watching over me.

CHAPTER TWO

In 1987, after two decades of digging at Tel Dan, Avraham Biran told an interviewer that he would dig for just one more season before settling down to write his final excavation reports. "By that time," he predicted, "I think we'll have done enough." Wise he may be, but no prophet—at least not in this instance. Today Biran is still digging at Dan, with as much success as ever, and there is always more to learn.

In this vibrant interview, Biran discusses some of his major finds, the problems that face archaeologists trying to reconstruct the past, and the relationship between archaeological artifacts and the Biblical text.

BAR INTERVIEW

AVRAHAM BIRAN
Twenty Years of Digging at Tel Dan

BAR Editor, Hershel Shanks, interviewed Avraham Biran, director of the Nelson Glueck School of Biblical Archaeology at Hebrew Union College, in Jerusalem.

Hershel Shanks: The name of Avraham Biran is—and will be for generations—inextricably bound up with the name of Tel Dan. When anybody thinks of one, he's inevitably going to think of the other. How long have you been excavating at Tel Dan, Dr. Biran?

Avraham Biran: It's very flattering of you to say, "For generations." But there's nothing really permanent, as you know. I suppose to be remembered for a generation or two, that's all one can really hope for. It is true, however, that Dan is probably the longest ongoing excavation in the country. We began at Dan in 1966. We have now completed our 19th season. We will have another brief season, which will bring us to 20. By that time, I think we'll have done enough; we'll have to sit down and put all the material together and publish the results.

HS: The word I get from the underground in Jerusalem is that you have had a very successful season this year.

AB: That's right, that's true. But I always wonder when we speak of a successful season, in what way is this season more successful than others? But if you refer to the discovery of unusual objects, then it's true.

HS: What did you find?

AB: Well, we found one unique object. You know the famous dilemma—an archaeologist always tries to find something unique and then he complains bitterly because he cannot compare it to anything else. So that is what happened to us in 1985. We found a little figurine on a plaque that we call in Hebrew—because it rhymes better than in English—*harakdan, mi-Dan*—the Dancer from Dan. We have the complete plaque with a man who's playing the lute and dancing. Of course, in Mesopotamia, north Syria, Egypt and Israel, we have found evidence of people who play an instrument. As a matter of fact, the lute that we have on our plaque looks very much like one of the lutes found in paintings from the Late

Bronze Age in Egyptian tombs. So the lute is not so unusual. What is unusual is the whole movement of the person. It is the

"Dancer from Dan" *kicks up his heels while accompanying himself on the lute.*

The unique clay plaque, about four and a half inches tall, dates to the 14th-13th centuries B.C., when a sizeable Canaanite settlement, called Laish in the Bible, existed at Tel Dan.

The Bible records that the Israelite tribe of Dan conquered the Canaanite city of Laish and renamed it Dan (Joshua 19:47; Judges 18:29)—an event Avraham Biran, Dan's excavator, dates to approximately the 14th century B.C.

The purpose of the plaque remains a mystery. Biran speculates that it may depict a dance not unlike the one David performed before the Ark of the Covenant when it was returned after having been captured by the Philistines (1 Chronicles 15:29).

Alternatively, the tile may have belonged to a guild of dancers and lute players or may even have served as a simple home decoration.

combination that is unusual. You have someone playing the lute, then you have the movement of the legs and the feet, which appears a little bit European or Aegean. The dress looks North Syrian or Canaanite. The face is very curious. Maybe the man wears a mask; on the other hand, it doesn't look like a mask. It looks a little bit like a satyr. This whole combination is indeed very unusual. We haven't been able yet to find any parallels with which to compare it.

HS: When do you date it? And what do you think its significance is?

AB: The dating I think is fairly accurate because we found it right beneath, or together with, a stone floor that extended out into a larger area which is dated to the Late Bronze Age.

HS: About 1300 B.C.?

AB: I would say around 14th-13th century B.C. But the question is: What is it? I have been trying to sort out some ideas, naturally.

HS: What are some of them?

AB: Well, the first thing that comes to mind is the Biblical account of David dancing in front of the Ark when the Ark was brought back from the Philistines to Jerusalem [1 Chronicles 15:29]. Now, of course, our plaque is a few hundred years earlier than David. But maybe our plaque depicts an event like this. Maybe there was a guild of dancers and lute players and this belongs to them. Or it may be just a decoration that was used in someone's house who collected such things.

We found this plaque when we were actually trying to find something else. Last year, 1984, when we were digging in that area, we were getting to the bottom of what we call a settlement pit of the Israelite period, and we came to the top of a structure that seemed to be a tomb. Large basalt slabs were set together to form a roof or ceiling of a structure underneath. We made this discovery, as often happens on an excavation, the last two days of the dig. Everybody got very excited, said "C'mon let's open it up, let's see what's in there." We were able to peer through the cracks in the stones. At the northern end of the structure we saw vessels. That seemed to indicate it was a tomb. Although everybody said "C'mon, let's excavate it," I said, "No. We don't have time." We didn't want just to open the structure; we wanted rather to open up a larger area in order to understand the relationship between this tomb, if it was a tomb, and the houses surrounding it. And that was what we actually did in 1985. We opened up a larger area and in the course of that excavation, we came across a stone pavement, and that's where we found the plaque with the dancer.

We still went down to find out about the

"An archaeologist always tries to find something unique and then complains bitterly because he cannot compare it to anything else . . . ."

tomb, however. From the top it looked like a very large structure, about six and a half meters [20 feet] long, with very fine stone slabs. We eventually entered the structure. Again, this happened toward the end of the season—and we found there four vessels, two oil lamps, a little jug and two bowls, all from Middle Bronze II [c. 1700 B.C.]. But there were no skeletal remains. That again raises some interesting questions: How come? Maybe it's not a tomb. Everybody started thinking and coming up with theories as to what it could possibly be. The most logical thing is to assume that it was built as a tomb, the offerings were put in, but for some reason—perhaps they didn't have time—or for whatever reason—they didn't bury anybody in there. And they closed it and blocked it from the outside. This is another one of those mysteries. Very intriguing.

HS: Let me come back to the plaque. You said it was Late Bronze. That would be the period just before the Israelite tribe of Dan conquered the city. At that time the city was called Laish, according to the Bible (Joshua 19:47; Judges 18:29).

AB: Right. That's very interesting that you should mention that because just now we've been trying to date the conquest of Laish by the tribe of Dan on archaeological grounds. As you know, there is a long

detailed account in the Bible about the Danite spies who were sent to Laish and how the Danites moved up and conquered the city, and so forth. That dates around the 12th century B.C. We are trying to establish a certain sequence between the Canaanite city and the Israelites. We did discover what we call the "Mycenaean" tomb—it wasn't really Mycenaean. We only called it Mycenaean because there were fantastic Mycenaean imports in it, such as the beautiful charioteer vase, which is quite unique in this country. We all had the feeling that the contents of this tomb represented the height of Canaanite civilization, just before the city was conquered by the Israelites.

HS: But you didn't find the Canaanite city itself. You found only the tomb. You didn't find the Canaanite city, did you?

AB: Ah, there is something archaeologists should be very, very careful in drawing conclusions about. There is a theory going around that there weren't many Late Bronze Age cities in Israel. There are even some doctoral dissertations written on the subject, about how little there was at the end of the Late Bronze Age in Israel. I came out with a statement years ago saying that if we had not found the Mycenaean tomb we would have to conclude that there was hardly any Late Bronze Age occupation at Laish at all. But if we had such a tomb, there must be a city. But we couldn't find it. This year, along with this Dancer from Dan [from the Late Bronze Age], along with this [Late Bronze] floor, this [Late Bronze] stone pavement, we also found remains of walls and structures that indicate that there was quite a city here during the Late Bronze Age. Why didn't we find it sooner? I think I have the answer: Everywhere we've been digging we came across these Israelite settlement pits. The Danites were a semi-nomadic tribe. As a matter of fact, the Bible refers to *mahaneh* Dan, the camp of Dan, when they were moving from the south to the north.

When they conquered Canaanite Laish, as the city was then called, they began a very slow process of urbanization, because the thing that strikes you at Dan is the many pits that were used for storage. Just this year we concluded that there were two types of pits. There were large pits, some of them stone-lined, which I think we might call community or clan storage pits. Then there were small pits, perhaps for families. While digging these pits, the Danites destroyed the remains of the city that existed before. It is indeed remarkable to find a few walls here and there. Now we have found this very fine stone pavement that extended over a large area and some walls, and we are convinced that there was

Stained with soil *from this 3,700-year-old "tomb," Biran (above) inspects two almost-intact pottery vessels, upper right, still half-buried in the floor.*

Oddly, the Middle Bronze Age II B (c. 1700 B.C.) structure yielded no skeletal remains, casting doubt on the structure's identification as a tomb. Biran speculates that the builders of the 20-foot-long building, roofed with massive basalt slabs visible at the top of the picture, may not have had time to inter anyone before some circumstance led them to seal it from the outside. Biran also speculates that it may have been a cenotaph, a tomb-like monument commemorating a dead person who was buried elsewhere.

In all, excavators uncovered four pottery vessels (right), two oil lamps, a small jug and two bowls from the ancient enclosure.

quite a large city of the Late Bronze Age at Laish.

HS: Those pits would not destroy pottery sherds from the Late Bronze Age, would they?

AB: No, but it would upset the archaeologist completely. Last year, we had a supervisor who was not well acquainted with the pottery. He was "reading" the pottery from Iron Age levels (the Israelite period), and assumed it was all Iron Age. I came in and saw that there was Late Bronze pottery. So we did find some Late Bronze Age material, just a few sherds. Then, as we went down still further, the pottery was clearly Iron Age. This supervisor said to me, "Well, how can that be? You told me yesterday that we had Late Bronze. And

suddenly we have Iron Age pottery below it?" That is against everything he had studied in college. But it became clear that the Late Bronze sherds had been taken out and thrown up when the Israelites dug the pits.

In these pits we found large collared-rim jars. I believe, with Albright, that these collared-rim jars were introduced into the country by the Israelites. Dan is an example of how this happens. There were no collared-rim jars at Dan during the Canaanite period. Suddenly they appear when the Israelites conquer the city.

HS: You say you didn't find collared-rim jars from the pre-Israelite period. But that may be because you found very, very little of anything from the Late Bronze Canaanite

city. You have been excavating here for close to 20 years; in the first 16 or 17 years all you managed to find of the Canaanite city that preceded the Danite conquest was an accidentally uncovered Mycenaean tomb. If it hadn't been for that tomb, you would have found almost nothing from the Late Bronze Age, from Canaanite Laish. The people who read **BAR** hear all the time that there was no city at Jericho at the time of the Israelite conquest, and that there was no city at Ai, although the Bible says the Israelites conquered it. These people are bound to wonder. Should they conclude that the Bible is wrong, or should they conclude that maybe the archaeologists are wrong? Here at Dan is another instance that seems to fit into this pattern. Here you

©HEBREW UNION COLLEGE/JEWISH INSTITUTE OF RELIGION

Collared-rim storage jars, *a distinctive feature of Iron Age Israelite material culture, were discovered in Danite "settlement pits" at Tel Dan. Traditionally, the jars are so named because of the rolled ridge around the shoulder of the vessel.*

The pits, dug by the seminomadic Danites as storage receptacles, may solve one of Dan's most perplexing mysteries: Why are there so few remains of the Late Bronze city called Laish, said to have been conquered by the Israelite tribe of Dan?

Biran suggests that the pits, dug into the earlier strata of occupation, have partially destroyed the Late Bronze Age occupation levels. The excavators uncovered more than 20 pits in one area alone—some as deep as six feet.

have no, or almost no, Late Bronze material and then suddenly, well, you have the tomb, you figure there must be a city. And now after 17 or 18 years you're finding evidence of a city. How do you explain this?

AB: First, allow me to make a slight correction.

HS: Please.

AB: There were always some Late Bronze remains at Dan—in Area A, in Area Y, in Area B, there are vessels and pottery from the Late Bronze Age. As a matter of fact, two or three years ago we discovered a whole building. It's true, the building is not from the end of the Late Bronze Age, but closer to the beginning of the Late Bronze Age. So although we didn't find a complete city, we do have Late Bronze remains.

When you talk about Jericho and other Late Bronze Age cities, people always think of city walls. "Where are the city walls, the fortifications?" they ask. Now I've always maintained—with respect to Dan, and I think it may be true for Jericho as well—

that what we found at Dan, the Middle Bronze Age rampart, the huge, so-called Hyksos fortifications, may help solve the dilemma. When the Israelites came, they encountered these Middle Bronze Age fortifications which were still being used in the Late Bronze Age. These were formidable fortifications. If we don't find Late Bronze Age walls, it's because the Middle Bronze Age fortifications served as a defense system in the Late Bronze Age as well.

HS: That was [Yigael] Yadin's view, too, wasn't it? About Jericho as well as Dan?

AB: I think so, and I think he was quite right. We have known about Dan from the beginning. When we began the excavation, we found an Israelite wall and an Israelite gate at the foot of the Middle Bronze Age rampart. This Israelite gate dated to around the ninth century B.C. so that it looked like there was no fortification of the city between the Middle Bronze Age [18th-17th centuries B.C.] and the days when Jeroboam set up the golden calf at Dan [at the end of the tenth century B.C.].

So the problem of the Late Bronze Age at Dan is not only the absence of a city, but also the absence of fortifications. Now we did have evidence of the Late Bronze Age here and there. We found Israelite settlement pits years ago. It took us about ten years to come to the conclusion that we had a lot of Israelite settlement pits. It wasn't so clear until we opened up a larger area. These past two seasons have convinced us that there were so many of them, one next to the other, that they destroyed much of the Late Bronze Age stratum. Obviously if you dig a pit and you excavate a wall, you remove it. That's what the Israelites did when they dug their pits. I think there was quite an important Late Bronze city here. The fact that we have the Mycenaean tomb from the Late Bronze Age

and the fact that we have the Dancer from Dan from the Late Bronze Age indicate a very developed civilization. And then after that level—above it, stratigraphically—comes a complete change in the material culture of the settlement.

Some have suggested a continuation of the Canaanites into the Iron Age. But why should the people of a highly developed civilization [the Late Bronze Age people] suddenly leave its high-class city and move into tents and huts and dig pits for disposal and storage? It just doesn't make sense. The change must reflect the coming of the Israelites and the displacement of the Canaanites.

HS: You called them "settlement pits." Are these strictly for storage or do you think people lived in them?

AB: No, they're definitely for storage.

HS: You have a great deal of evidence of the Israelite occupation of Dan. But you don't have any evidence of the destruction of the Canaanite city, do you?

AB: That depends on what you call destruction. The archaeologist is always very fond of saying when he discovers a good layer of fire, "Ah, that was a good destruction." He doesn't think of the poor people who died

Dwarfed by an earthen rampart *nearly 4,000 years old, an excavator stands on steps, leading from the western or interior arch, top center, of Dan's 18th-century B.C. gateway into the city below.*

Puzzled by the absence of Late Bronze Age fortifications around the 50-acre site, Biran suggests that the Middle Bronze earth ramparts surrounding the city continued to defend the Canaanite city of Laish through the Late Bronze Age and at the time of its conquest by the tribe of Dan.

The gateway complex, part of Laish's massive city defenses, was composed of three arches: an exterior, or eastern arch, facing outside the city; a center arch; and an interior, or western arch (artist's conception, inset), facing the interior of the city. The complex was flanked by two mudbrick towers extant to almost 20 feet, nearly their original height. Miraculously, the fragile mudbrick arches and gate complex survived intact through the centuries thanks to protective layers of soil. The Canaanites, for some unknown reason, decided to bury the gate complex by filling the gateway and covering the entire structure with earth, incorporating it into an earthen rampart around the city. Although this gate could no longer serve the inhabitants of the city, other gates were no doubt available. Such a large city would naturally have had more than one gate. As a matter of fact, Biran has found archaeological evidence for another gate at the southern side of the city.

in that destruction, but he collects all the vessels that he found in that destruction. We have one destruction from the middle of the 11th century B.C. that we connect with that very famous passage in the Book of Judges [19:31] about the temple or the sanctuary of the Danites that existed, "As long as the house of God was at Shiloh." In other words, Dan was destroyed at around the same time that the sanctuary at Shiloh was destroyed. The archaeological evidence for this level of destruction at Dan is dated to the middle of the 11th century, the date of the destruction of Shiloh. Now I do not suggest that the Philistines, who destroyed the sanctuary of Shiloh, were responsible for the destruction of the sanctuary at Dan. But the Shiloh destruction was of such magnitude and left such an impression that the people who wrote the Bible connected the destruction at Dan with the destruction at Shiloh.

HS: But the destruction of Dan you are talking about was long after the Israelites settled there.

AB: Yes, of course. That destruction occurred after the Danites had become urbanized.

HS: How far back does a sanctuary go at Dan? Was this a Canaanite sanctuary? Was Dan a holy site even then?

AB: That's a good question, penetrating—like all your questions. And embarrassing! Why did Jeroboam set up the golden calf at Dan? Was he looking for a site with a tradition of a sanctuary, a place that already had a tradition as a holy site? As you know, Jeroboam set up a golden calf at Bethel and at Dan [1 Kings 12-29]. Bethel is obviously the place where Jacob had his dream [Genesis 28:11-19] and there was already a sanctuary at Bethel. The name itself, Bethel, means the House of God. And so it was natural for Jeroboam to set up a sanctuary there. Bethel was also the southernmost city of the Israelite kingdom. Jeroboam also wanted a sanctuary in the north. But why at Laish/Dan? Just because it was in the north? The Canaanites perhaps already had a sanctuary there. Although we didn't find the golden calf, we did find, I think, the sanctuary where it may have been placed by Jeroboam. We found the high place, or bamah, but we haven't found the Canaanite sanctuary. Nor, for that matter, the sanctuary established by the Danites. There are great lacunae in our explorations.

HS: You haven't removed the Israelite sanctuary to see what's underneath it.

AB: Well, no. We can't. I mean, we can, but I wouldn't. Similarly with the Israelite city gate. It's so massive—I'm referring to the high place—it's a structure that is built of fantastic masonry which is similar to the masonry of the royal palaces at Megiddo and

Gezer and Hazor.

HS: Do you know what lies under that sanctuary, that bamah?

AB: No, I don't. But I would imagine if there is a Canaanite sanctuary it lies towards the center of the mound and not so close to the edge where the Israelites built their high place. The water level here is too high. We found a Late Bronze Age bowl in the area of the Israelite high place, but we were digging in mud, in water. Either the water table has changed or the system of drainage in antiquity was better than it is in modern times. We talked about bringing pumps and pumping the water, but I don't think it would help because I think it's a spring. In other words, we would be pumping the spring.

As for the Israelite sanctuary, it extended over a larger area than we supposed. That became clear this past season. In 1984 we excavated a large structure we call the lishkah, or chamber. We know about such chambers in sanctuaries from the Biblical account of the Jerusalem Temple, which mentions leshakhot, or chambers, as the King James Version translates it. There the priests officiated and their garments and the like were deposited. One of the walls of this lishkah at Dan extends 18 meters [nearly 60 feet]. There was only one entrance to it—from the east. At the end of this structure we found two tables, very well plastered, which may be offering tables. This season we decided to continue digging here. And we found the continuation of the building. They probably also built a terrace for a lower level of the building; here we found a square stone structure a little bit over three feet on each side. Of course we asked ourselves, "What is this?" One suggestion was that it is the base of a pillar that holds up the roof. Others suggested that maybe it's an altar.

We are always being criticized by Biblical scholars for taking a Biblical term and applying it to an archaeological object. So I am very cautious. Should I call it an altar?

Then to the east we found a bronze bowl with beautiful lotus decoration. What was it used for? It could be anything. Perhaps part of the ritual. Then to the north of the altar, or whatever this structure was, we found what the King James Version calls a censer or a shovel for coal or for incense. We found two shovels together. They had a loop at the end to hang on the wall. Now, in many of the ancient synagogues of the third, fourth and fifth century A.D. you find a depiction of the Ark of the Law and beside it you find an illustration of a censer or shovel. I don't think before our discovery last season anyone ever found an iron shovel in Israel from the eighth century B.C. Not even the most anti-archaeologist

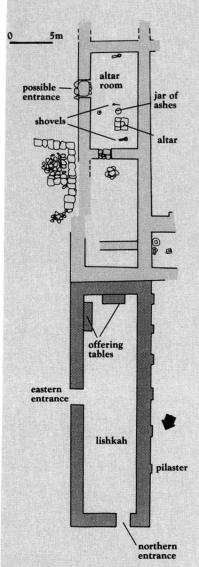

The Lishkah and Its Artifacts

Sixty feet long, this rectangular structu (right and plan, above) is apparently a eighth-century B.C. addition to the religious sanctuary at Tel Dan.

Jeroboam, king of the northern kingdom of Israel (924-903 B.C.), buil sanctuary at Dan to compete with the Temple in Jerusalem. As the Bible records, Jeroboam said, " 'Now the kingdom will turn back to the house o David; if this people go up to offer sacrifices in the house of the Lord at Jerusalem, then the heart of this peopl will turn again to their lord, to Rehoboam, king of Judah . . . .' So the king [Jeroboam of Israel] . . . made two calves of gold. . . . And he set one in Bethel, and the other he put in Dan" Kings 12:26-29).

Avraham Biran identifies the bamah,

or "high place" (see p. 33), as the focal area of Jeroboam's sanctuary. His recent excavation of the *lishkah*, however, revealed that the Tel Dan sanctuary is larger than he first supposed.

Students in the foreground of the photo (p. 31) clear the northern end of this *lishkah*, or chamber, where the priests may have officiated.

A three-foot-square stone structure

(top) found in the *lishkah* is an altar, according to Biran. A jar containing ashes was buried in the hole above the altar. The ashes have not yet been fully analyzed, but preliminary indications are that they may be frankincense and myrrh used in religious rites. Three iron incense shovels (bottom left), probably used during religious rites, were discovered nearby. The shovels, called

matah and *naah* in Hebrew, are the earliest such shovels ever found and resemble incense shovels pictured on synagogue mosaic floors of the fourth to fifth centuries A.D. Also found in this area was a bronze bowl (bottom right) approximately six-and-a-half inches in diameter and emblazoned with a lotus design. The finds all point to the cultic character of the building.

Biblical scholars can deny that these shovels are connected with cultic rites. Then to the southeast of the altar—or structure—we found another shovel. So now we have three shovels. To compound the excitement, we found a jar sunk into the ground full of ashes. These ashes are now being investigated by the laboratory. We haven't gotten the report yet. But I think there's no doubt that we are now in a chamber or in a room with an altar, probably an incense altar. Remember that the kings always offered incense. Some also made larger sacrifices of animals, but I think most of the time the kings would offer incense in the sanctuary, so we now have, I think, a sanctuary from the eighth century B.C., or maybe even a little earlier, around 800 B.C.

HS: That raises another problem for me. I noticed a time skip. We talked about the problem of the sparseness of Late Bronze Age material just before the conquest by the tribe of Dan. And now you discussed a lot of Israelite material. You have the building of the Israelite city and then you described this exciting sanctuary from perhaps as early as 800 B.C. Time and again, I find archaeologists talking about an enormous amount of material from these periods—the eleventh century and the ninth century, as you have done—but you've skipped something. You've skipped

the period of Israel's greatest glory, of its greatest empire, its expansion, power, authority—the period of the United Kingdom of David and Solomon, the first half of the tenth century B.C. Now where is that? What happened?

AB: You said it bothers *you.* Well, it bothers me more.

Fifty years ago I went looking for Anatoth, the city of Jeremiah. Near Jerusalem is a village named Anatha which obviously is the same name; Anatha is Anatoth—about this there is no question. Way back in the 1930s, Albright and Albrecht Alt surveyed Anatha, but they could not find any pottery from the Israelite period at Anatha. It was all Roman and Byzantine. Albright suggested way back then, when I was a young student, that we dig a site called Raŝ el Kharrûbeh near Anatha, where there were Iron Age remains. I did that. But I was not happy with what I found. There was very little from the seventh century [the time of Jeremiah], none from the days of David and Solomon—which you mentioned before—although the Bible also mentions Anatoth in that time. Anatoth was a levite city; priests came from Anatoth, according to the Bible. I suggested in a manuscript I submitted to Albright that we have to look for Anatoth elsewhere. Albright, in his inimitable way, published

Israelite "high place." *Volunteers armed with trowels and brushes clear the monumental staircase leading to a raised stone platform referred to as a* bamah, *Hebrew for "high place."*

The bamah, *the central cult site of Israelite Dan, dates from the end of the tenth century B.C. and continued in use to the eighth century B.C., the period of the Divided Monarchy. Biran suggests that the* bamah *was part of the religious sanctuary built at Dan by Jeroboam.*

Thus far no trace of the famed golden calf that Jeroboam erected at Dan (1 Kings 12:29) has come to light. Biran suspects that earlier Israelite and even Canaanite shrines may remain buried somewhere beneath the later structures of the cultic enclosure, or temenos.

my article but added a footnote saying I was all wrong. Okay, no harm in that. Fifty years later I went back to Raŝ el Kharrûbeh, but again I did not find any substantial evidence, not even from the seventh century, let alone from the tenth century. Not far from this site is a place called Khirbet es Sid where we found a large city of the seventh century. I've come to the conclusion that this is the Anatoth of Jeremiah. But the question remains, where is the Anatoth of David and Solomon?

There's something very interesting in the surveys that are being conducted these days. You find a very large and rich and intensive occupation of the hill country in the seventh century B.C., eighth century B.C., and very little of the days of King David.

We have this problem, even in Jerusalem. Nobody will say that Jerusalem was not occupied in the days of David and Solomon, at the time of the United Kingdom. Yet there is very little archaeological evidence for it. It's a very interesting archaeological-historical problem you're raising. There's no question that a city was there, at Dan, at the time of David and Solomon, but we haven't found it.

We have found a gate from the ninth century, possibly end of the tenth. In the ninth century, when Ahab obtained trade rights in Damascus [1 Kings 20:34], Dan was a very large city with a magnificent city gate, which we found. We also found the city walls. From a subsequent period, we found an upper gate—also from the eighth century B.C. Below the ninth-century gate is a fortress of the eleventh and tenth century. We have at Dan a fortification—perhaps what the Bible calls a *migdol* or a "tower sanctuary." There is no doubt in my mind that the city was fortified at the time of David and Solomon.

This past year we also found evidence of a metal industry—crucibles and tuyères from this period. Until about two or three years ago, we would have dated this to the tenth century B.C. This year we found these tuyères in quite a large area near the fortification which preceded Jeroboam and Ahab. And to top it all, not far from where we found the Dancer from Dan, we also found a piece of a crucible and tuyère from the Late Bronze Age. In other words, you have a metal industry at Dan from the Late Bronze Age to at least the ninth century.

Let me digress. I belong to what I think is the last remnant of Biblical archaeologists that are so much derided and spoken against in America. Now we know that the king of Tyre sent Solomon experts to help build his Temple. Hiram, the king of Tyre, sent Solomon a man he describes as a very wise person who knows how to work in gold and silver and stone and everything else. Then Hiram adds a cryptic statement: This man's mother comes from Dan [2 Chronicles 2:13]. Now why should he say that? Hiram is not interested in the question of, "Who is a Jew," which is engaging the attention of the Orthodox today. I think Hiram was telling Solomon "I'm sending you a man, an expert as a result of a long tradition of metalworking. He comes from a tribe that is known for its metalworking ability."

HERSHEL SHANKS

"The archaeologist is always very fond of saying when he discovers a good layer of fire, 'Ah, that was a good destruction.' He doesn't think of the poor people who died in that destruction . . . ."

That's why he says this man's mother comes from Dan. As a matter of fact, we know from the Mari tablets that Zimri-Lim, king of Mari, in the Middle Bronze Age, in the 18th century B.C., sends tin necessary for the manufacture of bronze to Laish/Dan. So you have a complete picture from the Canaanites down to the Israelites for this metalworking tradition at Dan.

HS: Well, the evidence that you've accumulated for me indicates that there was a city you found from the period of the United Monarchy, from the time of David and Solomon.

AB: Oh, yes, no question about it.

HS: But what about walls and pottery for this period?

AB: You see, the difficulty that we have is that later people destroyed so much of the earlier remains. When the Danite spies came back to report on the Canaanites, they reported a secure people were living in Laish. Why were they secure? The people of Laish felt secure because they used the walls and defenses from the Middle Bronze Age. They were so sure that nothing would happen to them.

HS: I'm not talking about a city wall; I'm talking about houses. Even secure people had houses with walls.

AB: We found destroyed houses in Level V,

a lot of houses. That's the 11th century. That level was destroyed in a great fire. That's just before the days of Saul and David and Solomon. In Level IV the houses had the same plan as Level V. As a matter of fact, the people of Level IV must have used the same walls; they just added to them; they raised them higher. Then we have the high place and sanctuary.

HS: That's a little later than Solomon, isn't it?

AB: All right, immediately afterward. Jeroboam [who reigned just after Solomon] didn't go to a city that was nonexistent. He went to Dan because it was an existing city.

HS: You earlier mentioned William Foxwell Albright, probably the greatest Biblical archaeologist that ever lived.

AB: And a great man.

HS: You were a student of his, weren't you?

AB: I was his first Ph.D.

HS: When was that?

AB: I hate to tell you! That was 1935. You know the Jewish tradition of the *lamed vovniks*, the 36 righteous men by whom the world is saved. Nobody knows who they are. When one dies, he is replaced. Albright was one of them, the 36. Albright was great, a saintly man. Albright said that the purpose of archaeology is not to prove or disprove the Bible. Albright regarded the Bible as a book of divine inspiration that needs no proof. What Albright was trying to do was to see if whatever historical references, historical memories, that are contained in the Bible have any relationship to the archaeological finds. I subscribe entirely to what Albright said. Certainly archaeology is not here to prove or disprove the Bible. What archaeology does is to make the references in the Bible a reality. Archaeology gives these references some bones and flesh.

I attended a symposium a few years ago in which people were discussing Assyrian and Babylonian documents. They discussed every detail and every historical implication. I got up and asked the lecturer, "If the Babylonians and Assyrians still existed today, would you treat their documents in the same way that you are treating them in your discussion?" And he looked at me with a twinkle in his eye and he said, "I think I know what you're referring to." Sometimes, merely because the Bible exists and merely because people read the Bible, study the Bible and follow the Bible, then for some people it is automatically discredited. Why?

HS: Why?

AB: The five books of Moses continue for twelve verses after saying that Moses died. It is the orthodox belief that the five books of Moses were written by Moses, so how can he die and the book continue? Some

believers say that God dictated these verses to Moses and Moses, with tears in his eyes, wrote of his own death. Ibn Ezra, a medieval commentator, was a little bit of a liberal, you might say, or a little bit modern; he saw there was something wrong with this. So when somebody asked Ibn Ezra about those last 12 verses, he said, "In my opinion, Joshua wrote these verses."

But, we were talking about Dan. As you know, Dan is mentioned in the story of Abraham. After the four kings of the north took Abraham's nephew Lot prisoner, Abraham pursued them, the Bible says, "as far as Dan" [Genesis 14:14]. Now, Rashi, the great commentator of the late Middle Ages, knew his Bible well. And when he came to this passage he realized that in Joshua and in Judges it is said that the name of the city was Laish before the Israelite tribe of Dan conquered it. So how could Abraham go to Dan, as it says in Genesis he did. Rashi in his own inimitable way says, "God showed Abraham the future." How do we explain this, according to our modern way of thinking? We say that the scribe who copied the text saying Abraham came as far as Dan was aware that nobody knows where Laish is anymore. Who knows today where St. Petersburg is? People don't even know St. Petersburg was changed to Petrograd and then to Leningrad. Today everybody knows Leningrad. So the scribe said to himself, instead of Laish, I'll write Dan. That's what everyone knows it by.

That explanation may be correct or may not be correct. But from the archaeological point of view, there is a very interesting

A crucible with a nugget of copper slag still nestled in its hollow, and the remains of two tuyères—tube-like air vents for blast furnaces or forges—were discovered in the Iron Age strata at Tel Dan.

These—and similar finds from the Late Bronze Age—bear witness to a thriving metalworking industry at Dan from the Late Bronze Age to the tenth century B.C.—a finding that seems to accord with the Bible.

The Bible records that Hiram, the king of Tyre, sent to Solomon a "skillful and experienced craftsman" to help him construct the Temple at Jerusalem. The artisan, Hiram told Solomon, was "the son of a Danite woman" and "an experienced worker in gold, silver and copper" (2 Chronicles 2:13,14). Hiram's boast of the workman's Danite heritage suggests a well-known and long-standing tradition of expert metalwork at the north Galilean site, says Biran.

question: If the Bible refers to Abraham coming as far as Dan/Laish, you can ask, "Was it a city or was it a myth?" There's no doubt in my mind that the city gate of the Canaanite period at Dan, the famous gate with the arches, was in existence. It was built around the middle of the 18th century, 1750 B.C. And there's no doubt in my mind that when a chieftain such as Abraham, who wins a great victory against the four kings of the north, comes to Laish/Dan, he would be met by the king of Laish. Can you imagine the king of Laish not going out to greet him, to meet him and to invite him to enter the city? From the archaeological point of view, I can only say, in the

18th century B.C. there was a city there with formidable defenses and with a fantastic city gate with arches and with steps leading up to it. Now of course if you say Abraham was not a historical figure at all, it doesn't make any difference. But if Abraham represents a historical figure and he comes as far as Dan/Laish in the 18th century B.C., then we uncovered the city he visited.

HS: So if Abraham existed and if he came to Dan/Laish, you have uncovered the gate he entered. Is that what archaeology is all about? Have you spent 20 years at Tel Dan to do that? What is the bigger significance of what you're doing? What kind of illumination are you providing? You're certainly not proving the Bible; you said that yourself. Nor are you disproving it. What is the bigger picture of what you're doing? What is the significance?

AB: You know, I just came back from a lecture I gave at the Explorers Club in New York. The members of the Explorers Club go to the North Pole, to the South Pole, they climb Mt. Everest. I was quite flattered that they invited me to give a lecture at the Explorers Club. I think I'm the first archaeologist to lecture there. And I began by asking the question you asked me: Why explore Dan? Why excavate? And I took a page from the honorary president of the Explorers Club, Edmund Hillary, who climbed Mt. Everest. When he was asked, "Why? Why climb Mt. Everest?" he looked at his questioners with surprise. "Because it's there," he replied. It's there—isn't that all that we're doing? Our country is dotted with sites. They're there. We want to know what's there, what's hidden there, what story they have to tell.

We went to Dan really as a rescue operation. The army was building fortifications in 1965, 1966, on the site, and there was a danger that whatever remains existed would be destroyed. We went there to see what we could salvage before all the archaeological remains disappeared. When we discovered in that very first year the Middle Bronze Age rampart, nobody knew what kind of fortification Laish had. But we did know a great deal about the site from the stories in the Bible. Not only in the Bible, but from the Egyptian Execration Texts that mention Laish. And from Mari (Zimri-Lim, king of Mari, mentions Laish), and from Pharaoh Thutmosis III who mentions Laish. It becomes intriguing. You have historical references outside the Bible and in the Bible. Would archaeology illuminate these references? Of course, it would be fantastic if we would find an inscription that mentions Horon Av, king of Laish. That is the name of the king of Laish in the Egyptian Execration Texts. But we haven't found such an inscription. What can I do? We haven't found the golden calf that Jeroboam placed there either. But still we want to know. We want to find out about the history of the country.

You ask me, "What is the big picture?" Let's go back to the collared-rim jars. They reveal very interesting "territorial history." That was a term used by Albrecht Alt—how the people moved and what culture they brought with them. Is it true that the tribe of Dan brought the collared-rim jars with them to Laish/Dan? And is the collared-rim jar a sign of the coming of the Israelites? Now it's true that Moshe Kochavi found collared-rim jars at Aphek from an earlier period, from the Canaanite period. And my colleagues in Jordan argued that there are collared-rim jars there and that therefore that doesn't prove they're a sign of the Israelites. But I say exactly the contrary. The Israelite tribes were east of the Jordan also. Historically, these collared-rim jars open up vistas.

You say I have been working 20 years at Dan and others are working elsewhere and what do we get? When I was studying under Albright and I despaired because Albright was such a genius and he knew so much, how could we even try to grasp anything; we students said to him, "Is there anything for us to do anymore?" That was in 1933, 1934. Albright replied, "You know, when I went to Jerusalem in 1920, I felt I had nothing to do. Everything had been investigated already. There was the survey performed by the British Palestine Exploration Fund, and there were other surveys." And Albright said, "You know, within a few months I just walked around Jerusalem and found new sites." He was so right. We have been working now so many years. It has now been a hundred years since Petrie excavated Tell el-Hesi [the first stratigraphic excavation in Palestine]. And still we haven't begun to scratch the surface. There is so much more to learn. So we have made mistakes, but we carry on.

HS: Some people say that the older archaeologists like yourself are not extracting as much as the younger archaeologists out of the material excavated. The younger archaeologists, some say, are using more modern, more advanced methods. How do you respond to that?

AB: I'll tell you, I feel young enough to consider myself part of the younger generation. And in my enthusiasm I think I can beat anyone of the younger generation.

HS: I wholeheartedly agree. How old are you Avraham?

AB: I'm 76.

HS: No kidding?

AB: No kidding.

HS: You act younger than I do, and I'm 55.

HERSHEL SHANKS

"The younger generation [of archaeologists] deals too much in details . . . . They don't draw general conclusions. But men like Albright and Breasted or Albrecht Alt could see the overall picture."

AB: You're a baby. I do agree that you have to use entirely new methods. So do we older archaeologists. And we do. When we find some metal, for example, those censers I mentioned, we showed them to Professor Robert Maddin from the University of Pennsylvania. Perhaps we or another scholar will research the metal and study it. When we found ashes in a jar next to the altar—years ago I would have thrown the ashes out. Now we save it and analyze it. Today everybody uses modern methods.

But I'll tell you: There is a difference between what you call the older archaeologists and the younger archaeologists. I think the younger generation deals too much in details. They do not see the forest for the trees. They don't see the whole picture. They don't draw general conclusions. It's not enough to say, "All right, there is so much percentage of gold in the bronze," and so forth. Now that's very interesting. In some of our bronze we found some gold in the tin, which comes perhaps from Great Britain. That's very interesting. Was there any connection, any relationship between Great Britain and this part of the world? But men like Albright and Breasted or Albrecht Alt could see the overall picture. We don't any more. They were trained in Egyptology, in cuneiform, in

Phoenician, in archaeology, in history, and in Bible and in philology. That's what enabled them to produce the kind of syntheses we really need in order to learn from the past. Some of us try to follow in their footsteps. But we can't. We don't have the ability, we don't have the knowledge. There's too much to know. And the younger generation knows much less. And they're abandoning the effort. And that, I think, is a shame. I have no doubt that they'll come back and make the effort to establish broader conclusions. You cannot stop with just the details. Otherwise, you're a mere technician.

A younger archaeologist came to me one day and said, "I'm going to publish a section." Ah! Wonderful! That's important! Really? I mean, if you draw a section of an excavation and you show the various levels, is that the answer to understanding the history of the site? A section is so arbitrary. If you had dug one meter to the other side of this section, you may get a totally different section. Sections *are* important. We use them. We have to. You cannot dig stratigraphically without them. But the section is not the beginning and the end. It is an instrument to understand. You yourself asked me: What about the houses? Where are the walls? How did they live? That is what we're trying to understand, the entire concept of the material culture of the civilization that existed. I think the younger generation will come back to that. In fact, they are beginning to do it, even now.

HS: You spoke about publishing a section. I suppose the greatest criticism I hear about you is that in 18 or 19 years of digging at Dan, you haven't published a real preliminary report. How do you respond to that?

AB: That is partially true. And I know that famous saying, "Publish or perish." But I don't think it's entirely true. We have brought to the attention of the scholarly world—and not only the scholarly world—everything that we have found. Some of it has appeared in **BAR.** Now it is true that we have not provided all the details that substantiate what we have found. But there are problems here too. You know in most textbooks I now find a drawing of the Israelite city gate of Dan, which was published in 1970 or thereabouts. I'm sorry now that I published that plan—because it's wrong. When we published it, that's what we had, but subsequently we discovered a major outer gate. There's always that danger if you publish too soon.

I'll tell you a secret: If we had stopped digging in 1966, '67, '68 or '69 and pub-

* See John C. H. Laughlin, "The Remarkable Discoveries at Tel Dan," **BAR,** September/ October 1981.

book. After that, we will work slowly to publish the details. I don't mean publishing 50 plates of collared-rim jars. You don't have to do that, and besides nobody can afford to anymore. You have to give the various types of collared-rim jars, but no one's going to learn anything by giving again and again and again the same one or the same cooking pot. You have to draw conclusions based on your evidence. And if scholars are going to be able to test your conclusions, you have to provide them with your material. That we shall do.

HS: Do you plan to publish a final report?

AB: A final report, yes, but I think that we're going to do it topically. I'll explain: We found a Mycenaean tomb. Everybody knows about the Mycenaean tomb; there have been some publications about it. True, we haven't published all the vessels that were recovered, so we'll do a monograph on the Mycenaean tomb. We've already published the three-arched gate from the Middle Bronze Age. Everything I know about that has already been published. I don't think I can add to that. The sanctuary, or high place, which again is another important item, has been published. So it's not entirely true, the accusation is not entirely justified, because the most important things have already been published. And these other things will come in due course.

HS: On a topic-by-topic basis rather than area-by-area?

AB: I think so. What I'm trying to do—and this comes back to your question about what we are learning. The "area" is arbitrary. I mean, after all, if I had dug, instead of Area A, let's say Area X, I might find completely different things. Because we have worked for so long, I think we can look at it in its entirety. The point of publishing is not Area B or Area T or Area A, in all of which we unearthed the Middle Bronze Age rampart, but rather what we know about the rampart together with the Middle Bronze gate that was found with the rampart. I think that would be more of a contribution in understanding the history of the site, the civilization of the people who lived there.

HS: Why are you stopping at 20 years of excavating Tel Dan? Because it's a round number? Because you're going to be 77 years old? Because you've done enough?

AB: All three together. We have to sit down. You see it's very difficult to start writing when you know you're going to have another season. So it's a good date, and if the good Lord will give us strength, then after we write for a year or two, perhaps we'll go back when I'm 80.

HS: May he bless you.

AB: Thank you.

lished the results, we'd have had an easy time. We'd know all the answers to all the problems that we encountered. But it would all be wrong. We are finishing next year, and then we'll sit down to produce first—I'll let you in on another secret: already we have what I call the pre-draft—not the draft, but the pre-draft—of a book on Dan.

HS: I know I've talked to you about doing a popular book on Dan. Are you talking about a popular book?

AB: It's not popular in a strict sense. It's a semi-popular book. "Popular" is the wrong word because it may imply that it's not scientific. But it will be a very readable

Charioteer vase. *This krater was just one of several Late Bronze Age Mycenaean imports uncovered at Dan in a well-built tomb that excavators dubbed the "Mycenaean tomb" because of its many Mycenaean artifacts. Other funerary offerings included gold and silver jewelry, bronze swords and ivory cosmetic boxes.*

The tomb and its contents may date to the heyday of Canaanite Laish and may bear witness to the city's prosperity and extensive trade relations before its destruction by the Israelites.

CHAPTER THREE

"Remarkable," "astounding," "almost miraculous"—
these are the words used by John Laughlin, a longtime member of the Tel Dan excavation staff, to
describe the finds that have emerged year after year
from the soil at Dan. And that's only on the first page
of the next chapter.

Among the most extraordinary discoveries reported by
Laughlin (now chair of the Department of Religion at
Averett College, in Danville,
Virginia) is this 4,000-year-old
city gate, with its arched entry-
way (opposite; model at left).

For uncertain reasons, the gate
was buried only 30 to 40 years
after it was built—leading to its
remarkable (there's that word
again) state of preservation.

THE REMARKABLE DIS

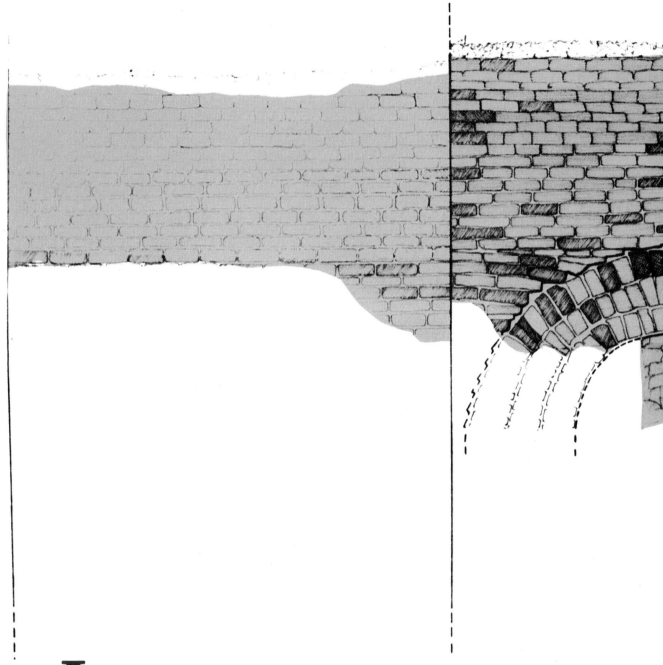

I N THE SUMMER OF 1979 an astounding structure was uncovered at Tel Dan in northern Israel. Excavators from the Hebrew Union College — Jewish Institute of Religion expedition found a huge mudbrick gateway consisting of two towers joined by a completely intact mudbrick arch. The complex is dated to the Middle Bronze II A-B period, about 1900-1700

B.C. The exact date is not yet known but it is probably earlier than 1700 B.C.

That the mudbrick towers were preserved to a height of almost 20 feet (very nearly their original height) was amazing enough. That the three courses of the mudbrick arch connecting these towers survived complete and undamaged after 3800 years seemed almost miraculous.

COVERIES AT TEL DAN

By John C. H. Laughlin

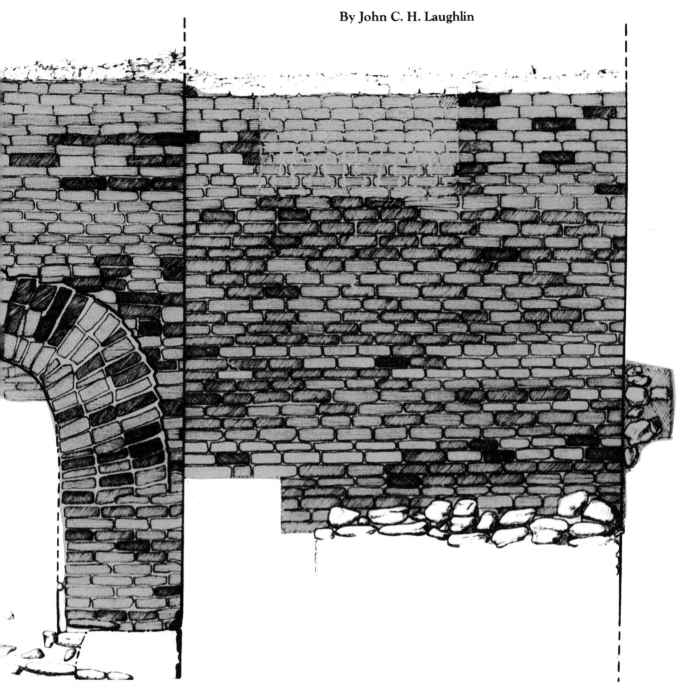

This is the only existing structure of its kind in the entire Near East. Remains of Middle Bronze gates have been found at Hazor, Megiddo, Shechem, Gezer and even Troy — but none of them is preserved intact. To find an entire mudbrick structure as old as the gate at Dan in this unbelievable state of preservation is hardly dreamed of by archaeologists.

The arched mudbrick gateway, built more than 700 years before the tribe of Dan captured the city, was preserved only because — for reasons not yet completely clear — it was *buried*. Whether the arched gateway can be preserved now that it is exposed to the air and the weather is a troubling question. (See the box on p. 56 for a recent report on the condition of the gate after its first

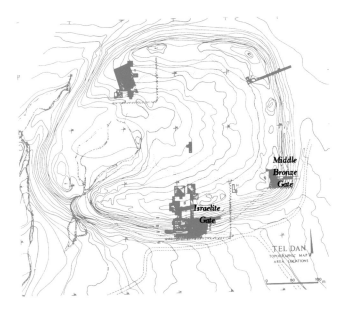

The Israelite (ninth century B.C.) gate at Dan is located on the southern slope of the tel about 175 meters (550 feet) to the west of the Middle Bronze (19th or 18th century B.C.) mudbrick gate. The relative positions of the two gates may be seen on the topographic map above.

Below is a plan of the Israelite gate. This gate is approached by a paved ceremonial entry road (see picture opposite) which passes through an outer and inner gate separated by an open paved area. Four guard rooms (A) and two main towers (B) comprise the inner gateway, measuring overall 29.5 x 17.8 meters (96 x 58 feet).

In the courtyard between the inner and outer gateways an unusual structure (C) was found built against the northern tower wall. The rectangular structure may have been the base for a king's throne or a cult statue. A close-up of this structure is seen on p. 44.

winter of exposure.)

No one was more surprised at the discovery of the gateway than Avraham Biran, head of Hebrew Union College's Nelson Glueck School of Archaeology and former Director of the Israeli Department of Antiquities. Biran has been director of excavations at Tel Dan since 1966.

How the gateway itself happened to be discovered at Tel Dan is a story in itself.

One of the most formidable features of Tel Dan — a 50-acre mound—is a massive rampart that surrounds most of the tel. Biran has expended enormous effort over the years trying to understand this rampart. Massive ramparts are common features surrounding Palestinian cities in the Middle Bronze Age. The rampart at Dan—or Laish, as it was then called—was by no means unique. It is generally thought that these ramparts were a defensive response to the invention of the battering ram. However, this is a much-disputed question; eminent archaeologists are still in disagreement as to just why these ramparts were built.

By 1978, Biran had cut through the Dan rampart at two places in order to examine its construction. From these two cuts, one in Area A at the southern end of the mound and the other Area Y at the northeastern end of the mound, Biran learned that the rampart consisted of an inner stone core which supported the outer slope on either side of the core. The earthworks thrown up against the stone core on the outside of the rampart consisted of alluvial soil from the surrounding plain. On the inside of the rampart, the builders built up against the stone core with soil from inside the city which included occupational debris from earlier periods. The base of the completed rampart, from one side to the other with the stone core in the center, was over 175 feet thick—nearly two-thirds of a football field. The stone core itself was over 20 feet wide and may have originally risen to a height of almost 60 feet above the surrounding plain.

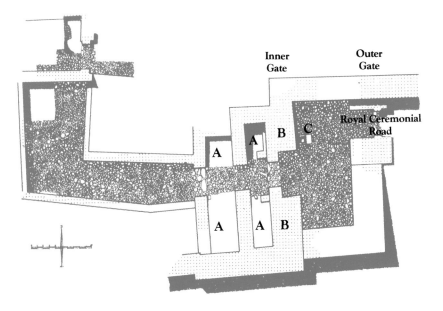

The paved royal ceremonial road led up to the east side of the ninth-century B.C. Israelite Gate. The pavement continued through the outer and inner gateways and into the city. This view is from outside the gate. The outer gate once stood about where the path is interrupted by low walls on the right. Against the wall in the background can be seen the podium pictured on p. 44 that once held the king's throne or statue.

The outer layer of the rampart was plastered with crushed travertine to prevent erosion of the slope. The plaster was not only impermeable to water, but it also stabilized a steep, smooth, hazardous slope which would cause an enemy to think twice before attacking the city. The builders of the rampart apparently considered a slope of about 40 degrees ideal.

In 1978, to check these conclusions, Biran decided to make a third cut into the rampart at the southeastern part of the tel, in what he calls Area K. In general, his earlier findings were confirmed.

At one point *within* the rampart in Area K, however, he came upon a mudbrick wall. His team of archaeologists and volunteers uncovered what they thought was a mudbrick wall which ran for a length of 30 feet in an east-west direction. Then the supposed wall turned south. This was all Biran knew at the end of the 1978 season. But this angle in the supposed wall was already enough for Biran to speculate that the structure might not be a wall but a tower—perhaps part of a gateway, he thought.

Subsequent excavation in 1979 proved him correct. What he had found in 1978 was the northern of two mudbrick towers which flanked the entranceway to Laish.

Did a king or a cult statue *sit on this platform within th Israelite gate at Dan? Round, carved, socketed bases sugg that posts were inserted in the holes to support a canopy ov the throne. Three of these round socketed bases can be seen the picture—two to the left of the platform and one on the right at the wall. A presumed fourth base has disappeared Behind the hewn limestone structure a bench protrudes fro the wall and continues five meters (16.25 feet) to the right until it meets the outer city wall. Perhaps it was of such a se that Samuel spoke when he said, "Then the king arose an sat in the gate" (2 Samuel 19:9).*

A massive rampart *surrounded the 50 acre city of Dan then called Laish—in the 19th-18th centuries B.C. The bas of the rampart was over 175 feet thick. Here, looking towar the outside of the city, we see a cut through the rampart. I the cut we may identify remains of the 20- to 25-foot stone core against which earthworks were piled on both sides. Th large boulders in the foreground are from an Early Bronz wall (about 25th-24th Century B.C.) which was reused in t later rampart. These boulders, as well as the smaller stone seen in the trench, are part of the rampart core.*

The mudbrick towers *of the Middle Bronze gate rested on massive stone foundations. Note the condition of the mudbricks both inside and outside the northern tower and the white plaster traces which remain from the original plaster coating of the tower. The remarkable preservation of these bricks for nearly 4,000 years can be explained by the fact that the entire gateway was buried shortly after its construction and incorporated into a huge defensive rampart which surrounded the city.*

In 1979 the tower was excavated to its base. It rested on a massive stone construction which guaranteed firm support for the mudbrick superstructure.

At the end of the 1979 season a staff architect was drawing a section of the just-excavated mudbrick structure. Suddenly he noticed that what he was drawing was the top of an arch. He immediately ran to the director with his drawing. Biran went to the site skeptically. How could a mudbrick arch be preserved for nearly 4,000 years, especially in a city that had seen as many wars and destructions as this one?

But Biran's skepticism turned to amazement as he examined the mudbricks *in situ*. The mudbricks had originally been covered with white plaster. The plaster had long since disappeared except in the joints between the courses of brick where it continued to adhere, seeming

An isometric reconstruction *of the Middle Bronze city gate at Dan.*

The face of each tower is approximately 16.5 feet wide, the same width as the center arched section. The entire width of the gateway is thus 50 feet. The center arched section is recessed 5.5 feet from the face of the adjoining towers. The arch spans almost 8 feet. The gateway complex is preserved to a height of approximately 20 feet, including 17 courses of mudbrick above the arch. This is probably quite close to its original height.

Traces of white plaster *adhere to the joints between the mudbricks in the Middle Bronze gateway. The curved white lines of plaster alerted the surprised archaeologists to the intact arched doorway, which they later excavated to its threshold. The wall protruding to the right of the arch is part of the northern gateway tower; the wall on the left edge of the picture is the bank of hard soil left in place to protect the unexcavated half of the gateway.*

to outline the bricks in white. The remains of the white plaster only emphasized the curve. There was no denying that an intact mudbrick arch had been discovered.

The next problem, which Biran postponed to the 1980 season, was how to excavate the arched gateway.

Sun-dried mudbrick begins to disintegrate as soon as it is exposed to air. It is one of the least durable materials that the archaeologist uncovers. But this was not the only problem with the mudbrick gate at Dan. At many places roots from trees on top of the tel had penetrated the mudbrick. Cracks were already visible in the part of the mudbrick tower exposed in 1978.

Another early concern was that the mudbrick arch might collapse. It turned out, however, that the Canaanites themselves had filled in the arched entranceway, thus supporting the arch, before burying the entire gateway

Only half of the arched *gateway was excavated, thus leaving a bank of hard alluvial soil on the left to support the mudbrick structure. Outside the gate, stone steps were uncovered which led down to the valley outside the city. The three steps, on the right, intersecting this stairway are part of a sloping stone revetment which prevented earth from sliding down the bank. Note that in this picture, as well as in the one on p. 39, the right half of the doorway has been unblocked; the archaeologists penetrated about nine feet into the gateway.*

structure within the rampart. By burying the gate within the rampart after only 30 to 40 years of use, the Canaanites unwittingly assured its preservation for nearly 4,000 years.

Biran finally decided to excavate the arched gateway in a very conservative way. He would leave half the gateway covered. The other half would be opened by digging a tunnel beneath the arch leaving a border of hard alluvial soil as a buffer between the supports of the tunnel and the mudbrick of the gate. In the summer of 1980 the gateway was penetrated by a tunnel almost six feet long. At its end the tunnel joined a guard room, to the right, within the tower. This room had previously been discovered when a deep shaft was sunk through the tower's mudbrick.

Outside the gate, the archaeologists uncovered steps that led to the valley floor below. Beneath these steps, at a depth of about one and a half feet, an earlier set of steps was found, clearly indicating that the gate had gone through at least two phases of use before it was incorporated into the rampart. This was subsequently confirmed by two thresholds which were found within the gate.

A number of questions about this remarkably preserved structure remain unanswered — perhaps we will never know the answers. Exactly when was the gate built? How long was it used? Why did the Canaanites stop using it? Why did they bury it within the rampart? How was the gate-tower complex connected to the city wall? In future seasons of excavation, Biran will be looking for the answers to those questions and others.

This unusual gateway is only the latest in a series of extraordinary discoveries at Tel Dan, including several which relate quite directly to the Bible.

As **BAR** readers know, Dan is mentioned frequently in the Bible. Originally, the city was called Laish (Judges 18:29) or Leshem (Joshua 19:47). When the tribe of Dan was unable to take possession of the territory allotted to it on the Mediterranean coast (Joshua 19:40-47), the Danites looked elsewhere for a place to live, finally settling in the city of Laish (or Leshem) which they conquered and renamed Dan (Joshua 19:47-48; Judges 18:27-29). Biran has identified the stratum VI city (about 1150

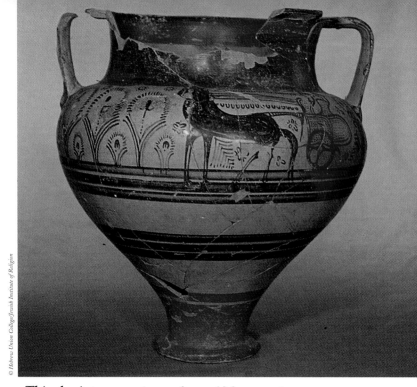

This charioteer vase *is one of several Mycenaean imports — including gold, silver and ivory objects — found in a magnificent tomb uncovered at Dan. This tomb dates from the Late Bronze period (14th-13th centuries B.C.) when a Canaanite city occupied the site. However, thus far, only this tomb has been found to suggest the size and prosperity of the Late Bronze Age city.*

B.C.) as the first Danite occupation.

This stratum consists principally of pits and stone-lined silos for storage. One of these silos was over six feet deep. Twenty-nine pottery vessels were found inside it, including large storage jars (*pithoi*) and cooking pots. Only one plaster floor was found, however. This archaeological evidence suggests that the Danites at first lived in tents or huts, which is consistent with the reference in Judges 18:12 to *maḥaneh Dan* or the tent camp of Dan. Only in the next level, Stratum V, did Biran find houses.

Interestingly enough, Biran has not yet found the Canaanite city which the Danites conquered. He has, however, found a magnificent tomb from that period, the Late Bronze Age (14th-13th century B.C.), which indicates that the Canaanite city, wherever it was (perhaps on the unexcavated western part of the mound), must have been large and prosperous. This unique tomb, known as the "Mycenaean tomb" because of the relatively large number of Mycenaean imports found in it, contained gold and silver jewelry, bronze swords, ivory cosmetic boxes as well as local and imported pottery. One of the Mycenaean pieces is a so-called charioteer vase, the only complete one of this type ever found in Canaan. The Mycenaean tomb contained 45 skeletons of men, women and children; apparently the bones and funerary offerings were periodically pushed aside to make room for new burials and offerings. Perhaps someday Biran will uncover the city where these long-buried people spent their lives.

Dan was the northernmost city of the Israelite tribal territories. During the Israelite monarchy Dan marked the northern border of the kingdom, which is frequently described in the Bible as extending "from Dan to Beersheba" (1 Samuel 3:20; 2 Samuel 24:15; 1 Kings 4:25; 1 Chronicles 21:2).

After the monarchy split in two after King Solomon's death in 921 B.C. and Jeroboam became king of the northern kingdom of Israel, he set up two religious shrines

The Sacred Area or temenos at Dan, seen behind the low wall in the foreground, was the cult place of the Israelites beginning in the tenth century B.C. Avraham Biran, director of the Dan excavations, believes he has found here the beth bamah or high place which was built by Jeroboam, King of the northern Kingdom of Israel, to compete with the Jerusalem Temple, as described in 1 Kings 12:29. The earliest bamah at Dan was an open-air platform approximately 22 x 60 feet; only two courses of stones remain from this structure. Some of these stones show the effect of the fierce fire which destroyed the structure. In the ninth century B.C. a second bamah was built upon the remains of the first and the platform was expanded to 60 x 62 feet. This bamah was constructed on finely dressed masonry which can be seen in detail on page 53. Nearby, in an adjacent courtyard, a horned incense altar (see p. 52) was discovered which may date from the period of the second bamah.

The third Israelite rebuilding of the bamah occurred in the first half of the eighth century B.C., when a 27-foot-wide monumental stairway (seen in the center of the picture behind the low wall) was built against the southern face of the platform. Below is an artist's reconstruction of this bamah.

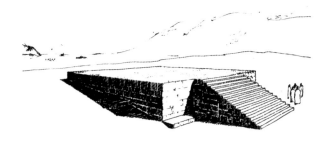

John Laughlin

Dressed stones *used to enlarge the high place in the ninth century B.C. (bamah B) are laid in a header and stretcher pattern. By alternating ends and sides in a row, the wall was given greater strength than if all were placed in a common orientation. This finely carved masonry resembles the masonry used in royal buildings of the same period at Megiddo and Samaria.*

A trident *decorates the bottom of this pottery bowl found at the Israelite sanctuary. The bowl contained bones of sheep, goats and gazelles which were probably sacrificed during rituals at the high place.*

A horned incense altar *found in a courtyard near the high place at Dan is almost perfectly preserved. It is about 16 inches high. Black burn marks on the top are clear evidence of its frequent use. This altar probably dates to the second Israelite bamah at Dan, in the early ninth century B.C.*

to compete with the Jerusalem cult. One shrine was at Bethel, on the southern border of the country and the other was on the northern border at Dan (1 Kings 12:29). In each shrine Jeroboam set up a golden calf. "Here are your gods," he told the people of Israel (1 Kings 12:28). He also set up altars and appointed priests to serve at the shrines, which are referred to in the text as *beth bamoth* (1 Kings 12:31). A *beth bamah* (plural, *bamoth*) has been variously translated as a hilltop shrine (New English Bible), a house on a high place (King James, Revised Standard Version, and Jewish Publication Society), a high place (Jerusalem Bible), and a cult place (New Jewish Publication Society).

High places were used for general worship purposes.[1] The most common religious practices mentioned seem to be sacrifices and the burning of incense (1 Kings 3:3; 12:32-33; 2 Kings 16:4; Jeremiah 19:3-5; Ezekiel 6:6; 20:28). In addition, people ate and prayed there (1 Samuel 9:13, 24). Biran believes he has found the remains of the *beth bamah* first constructed at Dan by King Jeroboam.[2] Although some archaeologists have questioned this bold conclusion, there is no doubt Biran has uncovered an impressive Israelite cult place.

The Sacred Area or *temenos* at Dan is a large complex over a half-acre in size. The central open-air platform of the Sacred Area went through three phases during the Israelite period. Biran has identified the three phases of the platform as Bamah A, Bamah B, and Bamah C.

Bamah A is probably the one built by Jeroboam in the late tenth century B.C. (This Jeroboam is known as Jeroboam I to distinguish him from a later Israelite king of the same name.) Bamah A consists of an open-air platform approximately 22 feet wide and 60 feet long constructed of dressed limestone blocks on a base of rough stones. Only two courses of Bamah A have survived. It was destroyed by a fierce fire so hot that it turned the edges of the stones red. From this phase of the sanctuary Biran found the remains of incense burners, a decorated incense stand, the heads of two male figurines, and a bowl decorated with a sign resembling a trident. The bowl contained fragmentary bones of sheep, goats and gazelles which had probably been sacrificed at the sanctuary.

During the first half of the ninth century B.C. the open-air platform was rebuilt and expanded into an almost square structure measuring 60 by 62 feet (Bamah B). The masonry of this bamah, including dressed stones with bosses laid in header and stretcher fashion compares well with the royal buildings from the same period found

An archaeologist's treasure—*a four-line inscription containing the name Dan*—*was uncovered in the sacred area. Not only does the ten- by six-inch tablet confirm the identity of the site, but it is also evidence that the area was a sacred site as late as the third-second century B.C., the date of the tablet. The inscription, three lines in Greek and the bottom line in Aramaic, refers to a person "Zoilos" who made a vow to the "god who is in Dan" or, an alternative reading, to the "god of the Danites." The Greek word for Dan appears as* **ΔAN** *in the second row.*

at Megiddo, and similar buildings from Samaria. This masonry is among the finest found in Israel.

A nearly complete horned incense altar was uncovered in an adjacent court which may come from this time period. The altar, with one horn perfectly preserved, is about 16 inches high and shows evidence of long use. We may assume that many of the activities associated with the bamah, including the burning of incense, took place in courtyards surrounding the open-air platform where this incense altar was found.

The third stage of the bamah's history (Bamah C) reflects the period of the first half of the eighth century B.C. At this time a set of monumental steps, about 27 feet long, was built against the southern face of the open-air platform. The upper three courses of these steps were added or repaired in Hellenistic or Roman times, indicating that this Sacred Area continued to be used for cultic purposes perhaps to the turn of the era. Other

evidence—additions to walls and new rooms—confirms this conclusion.

That the area remained cultic is also shown by a unique find dating to the Hellenistic period (third-second century B.C.) uncovered in the Sacred Area. In 1976 Biran uncovered a beautifully preserved votive inscription carved on a limestone slab approximately 10 x 6 inches. The inscription, three lines in Greek and one in Aramaic, refers to a person named "Zoilos" who made a vow to the "god who is in Dan" or—an alternative reading—to the "god of the Danites." Although the Aramaic portion of the inscription has been damaged it probably reads the same as the Greek.[3]

With the recovery of this inscription, Dan becomes one of a handful of sites whose identification is confirmed by finding the name of the site inscribed on an artifact found there. Gezer and Hazor are two other such places.

About 70 feet south of the open-air platform Biran found, during the 1978 and 1979 seasons, a unique cultic installation which apparently involved the use of water libations. There is nothing the least bit like it in the entire Near East. In the center of this unusual installation is a sunken base which rests on a lining of pavement stones. On either side of this plastered basin two large, flat basalt slabs were laid, one to the north of the basin, the other to the south. The slabs slope gently away from the basin. At the end of each basalt slab is a sunken jar embedded up to its mouth in plaster, with its mouth pointed toward the basalt slab and the basin in the center.

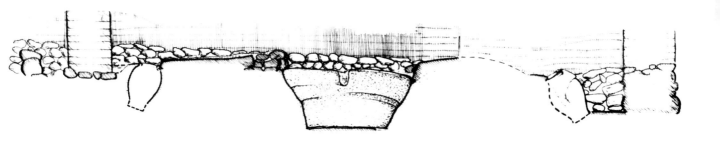

John Laughlin

A unique installation, *probably used in a water libation ritual, was discovered 70 feet south of the sacred area at Dan. The drawings show the components clearly: a central sunken basin flanked by two basalt slabs which slope toward the open mouths of two buried jars. The top drawing is a section, or vertical slice, through the center of the installation; the bottom drawing is a view from above. It is not known what purpose was served by the pile of small stones with holes.*

The 20-foot-long installation dates to the late tenth-ninth century B.C., the time of the divided monarchy in Israel.

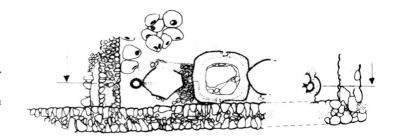

Mudbrick Gateway Deteriorating After Exposure

We regret to report that the magnificent intact mudbrick gateway which we feature on our cover no longer looks as it is pictured. As the archaeologists feared, the fragile mudbrick, although roofed to protect it from rain, began to crumble shortly after its exposure last summer. The stone steps leading to the threshold are mostly covered with soil from the disintegrated mudbricks and the ancient arch can be identified only by those who know where it is.

Fortunately, because of the excavator's foresight, half of the gateway remains buried and protected by the bank of alluvial soil which was packed against it almost 4,000 years ago.

Someday a technological solution will be found for the problem of preserving mudbrick — perhaps a coating, perhaps a chemical infusion. When that capability is achieved, other archaeologists may then expose the southern half of the Middle Bronze gate so that it may stand perfectly preserved, the way its other half was seen so dramatically last year.

The Biblical Archaeology Society Preservation Fund hopes to play a role in speeding the development of techniques for the preservation of mudbrick. But the problem is not easily solved.

An Egyptian pharaoh *wears the white crown of Osiris. This small fragment of a faience figurine was found in the southern jar of the cultic installation in the sacred area.*

A groove or slit in the southern slab was carved which may have directed the water (or other liquid) into the jar at the end of the slab.* A similar channel was carved in the plaster which covers the northern slab. This entire installation is 20 feet long and dates to the tenth-ninth century B.C., the period of the Israelite monarchy.

That ancient Israelites engaged in water libation ceremonies is clear from several Biblical passages.

When Samuel assembled all Israel at Mizpah to judge them, the Israelites "drew water and poured it out before the Lord and fasted all day, confessing that they had sinned against the Lord" (1 Samuel 7:5-6).

Elsewhere, we read of King David pouring out water to the Lord, water which had been brought to him by his warriors at the risk of their lives (2 Samuel 23:16). Ezekiel speaks of drink-offerings being poured out at high places (Ezekiel 20:28).

Unfortunately, the Bible gives us no more details of these ritual libations. How the water or liquid ritual at

---

* There are also other possibilities. The grooves appear to be too shallow to catch much water.

Dan was performed remains unclear. Probably the water was ladled from the basin and poured onto the basalt slabs and flowed from there into the jars. But more than this we do not know.

Tantalizing bits of evidence found with the water installation are difficult to interpret. For example, in the jars at the ends of the slabs, the excavators found pieces of greenish faience figurines. Other faience figurines were found nearby. The figurines reflect a strong Egyptian influence, but they were not made in Egypt. One of the figurine fragments is a head of an Egyptian pharaoh wearing the white crown of Osiris; another is a male head. Still another is a torso of an Egyptian man or god holding a staff or lotus flower. A final fragment is a monkey seated beside a standing figure holding a scepter or staff. These figurines were probably votive offerings brought to the high-place at Dan. But they do not tell us how the water system worked.

Equally mysterious are some stones found near the water installation, each with a hole pierced in one end. How were they used? We do not know.

In a room of a building near the water installation, Biran recently found a water channel which may have been used to bring water from the abundant springs in the area into the rooms for use in the water installation. If this can be substantiated in the continuing excavations, this would lend added support to the hypothesis that the early Israelites practiced a water purification or libation ritual at

An Egyptian man *or god holds a lotus flower before him. The small faience figure was found near the cultic installation at Dan.*

this unique Iron Age installation.

In any event it is clear that this entire area at Tel Dan was an important Israelite cultic center. Whether it is the *beth bamoth* referred to in 1 Kings 12:31, as Biran believes, will no doubt continue to be debated by scholars for years to come. Although the Biblical record is silent concerning the specific cultic acts performed at Dan and does not even specify what use was made of the Golden Calf which Jeroboam made, the archaeological evidence suggests that a large, open-air platform was used, that there were altars, incense offerings, votive offerings involving figurines, and some kind of water purification or libation rituals.

A sanctuary this large and elaborate would no doubt have attracted people far beyond the walls of Dan; this was the intention of Jeroboam I and the later kings of Israel who wanted to counter the powerful attraction of the Jerusalem cult. So Jeroboam "set one in Bethel, and the other he put in Dan. And this thing became a sin, for the people went to the one at Bethel and to the other as far as Dan" (1 Kings 12:29-30).

[1]See Roland de Vaux, *Ancient Israel,* Volume 2, "Religious Institutions," (McGraw Hill, New York: 1965), pp. 284-88.

[2]See most recently his "Tel Dan: Five Years Later," *Biblical Archeologist,* 43:175, 1980.

[3]See the discussion by Avraham Biran, *Israel Exploration Journal,* 26:204-205, 1976.

In this article, photographs credited to Hebrew Union College-Jewish Institute of Religion were taken by Avraham Biran and Ze'ev Radovan.

CHAPTER FOUR

The "last word" is seldom written in archaeology, as the following chapter reflects. When Biran uncovered a strange stone structure half buried in the ground, he interpreted it as a cult installation used in some kind of water libation ceremony. That opened a debate in the pages of *Biblical Archaeology Review*; two sharp-eyed, strictly nonprofessional readers contended that the "cult installation" was something more prosaic—simply an olive press. Two prominent scholars sided with the *BAR* readers. Biran and his colleague John Laughlin, however, stuck by their guns. And the last word has still not been written. Readers are free to make up their own mind.

The faience head of a pharaoh (opposite)—discovered inside one of the jars in the alleged cultic installation—may well know the answer to the puzzle. But, alas, he remains mute.

Is the Cultic Installation at Dan Really an Olive Press?

A DISCUSSION THAT STARTED IN **BAR** ESCALATES IN THE SCHOLARLY WORLD

IN THE PREVIOUS CHAPTER ("The Remarkable Discoveries at Tel Dan," reprinted from **BAR**, September/October 1981), John Laughlin identified an unusual installation at Tel Dan, in northern Israel, as an Israelite cult installation associated with a water libation ceremony. In explaining the installation as having been used in a religious water libation ceremony, Laughlin adopted the interpretation of Tel Dan's excavator, Avraham Biran.[1] The installation is dated to the tenth or ninth century B.C.

The unusual installation consists of three parts. In the center is a sunken basin whose rim is at ground level. The plastered sides of the basin slope inward. Flagstones cover the bottom of the basin. At ground level, the basin is flanked on either side with a basalt slab. Each of these basalt slabs slopes toward the third element of the installation—an open-mouth pottery storage jar sunken up to its mouth at the end of each basalt slab. Each jar is plastered around its open mouth.

In their discussions, Biran and Laughlin were not sure just how the installation was used in the water libation ceremony. Laughlin wrote: "Probably the water was ladled from the basin and poured onto the basalt slabs and flowed from there into the jars. But more than this we do not know."

A final mystery involved a pile of ten stones with holes in them found next to the cult installation. No purpose could even be conjectured for the stones.

The strange installation, framed by walls on three sides, was located at the far end of a room or courtyard. This room was just 70 feet south of the sacred area or *temenos* at Dan, an area Biran believes was the cult place of the northern kingdom of Israel from the time of Jeroboam I in the tenth century B.C., until the eighth century B.C. The central feature of the *temenos* was a large platform, described by Biran as a *bamah*.* Close by, in a court adjacent to the open-air platform, a nearly complete

horned incense altar (see p. 52) was found, probably dating to the ninth century B.C., when the *bamah* was rebuilt and expanded.

In a letter in the January/February 1982 **BAR**, Cathy and Terry Small of Berkeley, California, proposed that the Dan installation was not used for a water libation ceremony, but was part of an olive press.** The Smalls suggested that the central sunken basin was used for the initial crushing of the olives in the first stage of olive oil production. After the "first quality" oil was removed, the oil pulp could be bagged and further crushed "by pressing it beneath a heavy beam." This could have been done on the slabs on either side of the central basin. The olive oil removed in this way would have flowed down the slabs into the sunken jars at either end. The Smalls even had an explanation for the puzzling stones with holes in them: the perforated stones were weights to hang on the beam that crushed the bagged olive pulp. Both John Laughlin and Avraham Biran rejected the Smalls' suggestions. They did not believe the installation could have been used to press oil from olives.

Now, two scholars from the Oriental Institute at the University of Chicago have published the same suggestion made by Cathy and Terry Small, closely following the Smalls' argument. Although the article by Lawrence Stager and Samuel Wolff[†] appeared after the Smalls' letter was printed in **BAR**, Stager and Wolff reached

---

Bamah refers to a large open-air platform used for cultic rituals such as sacrifices. Sometimes a *bamah* is called a "high place."

**Independently, the same interpretation was offered by Oded Borowski in "A Note on the 'Iron Age Cult Installation' at Tel Dan," *Israel Exploration Journal* 32:1 (1982).

†"Production and Commerce in Temple Courtyards: An Olive Press in the Sacred Precinct at Tel Dan," *Bulletin of the American Schools of Oriental Research (BASOR)* 243 (1981). Although the date of the *BASOR* containing Stager and Wolff's article was 1981, the journal actually appeared in print in 1982. (Frequently scholarly journals fall behind in their publication schedules but continue to date issues according to the planned sequence.) Stager and Wolff's article was written late in 1981, as a result of hearing Biran present his ideas in Dallas in December 1980.

Olive press or cult installation? When this photograph first appeared in BAR, in the September/October 1981 issue, the enigmatic installation was tentatively identified by the excavators at Tel Dan as a site for water libation rituals.

Now, some archaeologists argue that the configuration of slabs, basin and buried jars is in fact the oldest olive press yet discovered in Israel, dating to the late tenth or the ninth century B.C.

The photo shows a sunken basin with plastered sides and a flagstone bottom, a flat basalt slab to its left and, far left, the open mouth of a buried jar. Not seen in the photo, but illustrated in the cross-section drawing and the plan (right), are another slab and buried jar to the right of the basin. (The top drawing is a view of an imaginary vertical slice through the center of the installation; the bottom drawing is a view from above.)

Here is how the installation would have worked as an oil press. First the olives were crushed in the central basin. Water was added to the pulp so that the lighter oil could be skimmed off the surface. The pulp residue was then placed in woven baskets that were stacked on the basalt slabs on either side of the basin. The remaining oil was pressed out of the pulp by the pressure applied by a long wooden beam. One end of the beam fit into a niche,

not visible in this photo, in the wall behind the pressing platforms. On the other end of the beam hung large stone weights, probably the perforated stones seen here behind the basalt slab. These weights caused the beam to press the stacked baskets with tremendous force, squeezing out the pulp's remaining oil, which then ran down the slanted pressing platforms into the open mouths of the buried vessels. (A similar beam press is illustrated on p. 63.)

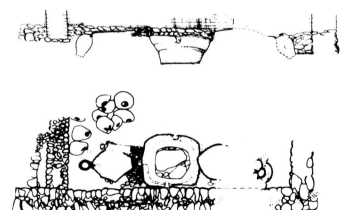

Tel Dan olive press. *No one argues with the interpretation of Tel Dan's excavator, Avraham Biran, that this stone slab was part of an olive press. The simple basalt structure is practically identical to many other presses excavated in Israel.*

Oil expressed from pulp stacked in baskets on this stone collected in the circular groove and then ran into the channel extending from the groove. The oil then dripped from the end of the channel into a collecting vessel that would have been placed alongside the press.

Biran claims that this press and the installation in the Dan cultic area are contemporaneous. He argues that the Israelites at Dan would not have built two different types of oil presses in separate parts of the settlement.

their conclusions independently, having written their analysis before the Smalls' letter was published in January 1982.

In Stager and Wolff's analysis, the perforated stones are a key element supporting the conclusion that the Dan installation is an olive press. "The stones are too large," they say, "to be loom weights or net sinkers. They vaguely resemble small anchors, but votive anchors at this landlocked site seem unlikely." Most likely, the two scholars conclude, the perforated stones were counterpoise weights for a beam or lever press. What would have been pressed? Stager and Wolff note that "since the substantial force that a beam press applies is hardly necessary to express juice from the grape, the olive remains the only obvious choice."

Like the Smalls, Stager and Wolff note that olive oil production is a two-step process: first, crushing the olive; then pressing the pulp to express the olive oil. The expressed oil flows into a channel leading to a vat or vessel. Stager and Wolff propose that at Tel Dan, the olives were first crushed in the central plastered basin to produce an oily pulp. Then, water was added to the pulp, causing the oil to rise to the surface, where it was

collected. Probably the pulp was then placed in baskets stacked on top of the basalt slabs for pressing. Each slab was serviced by its own beam press, with one end of the beam fixed in a notch in a wall to the west of the installation and with the other end hung with weights that pulled the beam down across the top of the stack of pulp-filled baskets. Oil expressed by the beam's pressure ran into the grooves cut into the basalt slabs and flowed into the underground storage jars, where it remained until it was ladled out.

If Biran's tenth- or ninth-century B.C. date for the installation is correct, then the Dan oil press is the earliest example known from Palestine. Other two-beam olive presses sharing a common crushing basin have been found from the eighth or seventh century B.C. at Gezer, at Tell Beit Mirsim and at Beth Shemesh. Recently, an almost exact parallel to the Dan installation was found at Tel Batash, a site identified as Biblical Timnah. Archaeologists George L. Kelm and Amihai Mazar reported[2] that, in the courtyard of a seventh-century B.C. pillared house, they found "an oil press containing a large stone trough and two stone vats built into a plastered stone platform." The excavators suggest that the crushed olives were placed in woven straw baskets over the open mouths of the vats. Then a beam with weights attached pressed on the stack until the olive oil dripped into the open vats.*

There is one striking difference between the Dan press and those presses at Beth Shemesh, Tell Beit Mirsim, Gezer and Tel Batash. The latter four presses were found in domestic/industrial contexts; the press at Dan—if that's what it was—was located in the *temenos* or sacred area.

The location of the alleged press at Dan—in an indisputably cultic area—was one of the reasons Laughlin rejected the olive press suggestion when it was made by Mr. and Mrs. Small: "That the inhabitants of the city would have engaged in such an activity as the making of olive oil in a sacred area is unlikely," he said.

Stager and Wolff make a special point of demonstrating that this location for an oil press may not be so incongruous as it first seems. Olive oil was widely used for ritual purposes in Biblical times. Moreover, "temple industries" have been found in cultic areas at other excavated sites.

* As **BAR** was about to go to press, a phone call from Trude Dothan, co-director of the excavations at Tel Miqne (Biblical Ekron), brought us news of yet another oil press, uncovered this past summer at Ekron. This one, dated to the seventh century B.C., is also the type with a central basin flanked by basins on either side. In addition, the excavators found perforated stones and charred wood from a beam. Nearby, Dothan reports, a small horned altar was discovered.

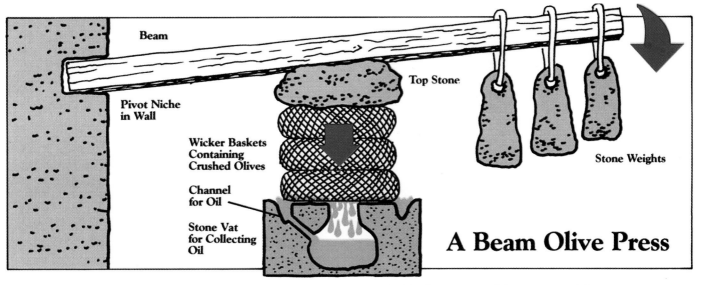

Beam

Pivot Niche in Wall

Top Stone

Wicker Baskets Containing Crushed Olives

Channel for Oil

Stone Vat for Collecting Oil

Stone Weights

A Beam Olive Press

We know that kings were anointed with olive oil at their coronations. Before the Temple in Jerusalem was built, this ceremony took place at the "tent-shrine" by the Gihon Spring in the City of David (1 Kings 1:38-39). We are not informed about the coronation ceremonies of the Israelite kings; it seems likely, however, that the service was conducted in Samaria rather than in either of the two religious centers, Dan and Bethel.

Although no evidence has been uncovered at Dan for even an occasional anointing ceremony, two other ritual uses for oil do suggest plausible reasons for having a permanent oil press in the *temenos* at Dan. These uses are libation offerings and fuel for sanctuary lamps.

Olive oil was used in the lamps that burned in the sanctuary. In the Tabernacle tradition, "pure oil of crushed olives" (*šemen zayit zāk kātît*) was prescribed for this purpose (Exodus 27:20; Leviticus 24:2). Only "pure" (*zak* [masc.], *zakkah* [fem.]) oil and frankincense were to be used inside the Tabernacle, the holiest sphere of the *temenos*; for sacrifices of oil and frankincense offered outside, in the court, this specification did not obtain. There was also the practical benefit of burning "pure" oil in the inner sanctum: the walls and curtains were less likely to be darkened with soot, because pure oil burns with an almost smokeless flame.

A number of ostraca found in eighth-century B.C. Samaria record shipments received of "washed oil" (*smn rhṣ*), probably vocalized *samn rāḥūṣ*). Stager recently wrote[3] that in all probability, *samn rāḥūṣ* is the north Israelite term for what the Bible refers to as *šemen kātît*, literally "crushed oil." In Biblical times, both terms referred to the finest quality oil.*

This finest quality oil came from the first crushing, done in a mortar or vat before pressing. By on-site inspection of olive oil production, the priests could guarantee the quality of fuel for the lamps. In the sacred area at Dan, terra-cotta sanctuary lamps set on high pedestals—including a seven-spouted variety—were

found. The *šemen zayit zāk kātît* expressed from olives in the Dan installation may have burned in such lamps after an on-site purity inspection by the resident priests.

According to the Bible, olive oil was also used to make cereal offerings on altars or in temple courtyards. The cereal offering (*minhah*), according to priestly tradition, consisted mainly of fine ground flour (*solet*) mixed with a high proportion of oil of crushed olives (Numbers 28:4-5; Exodus 29:40). Although the proportion of ingredients in the *minhah*-offering may have varied from time to time (cf. Numbers 28:4-5; Ezekiel 46:13-15), it seems likely that olive oil was always a primary ingredient, especially because of its combustible qualities.

At Dan, the olive oil manufactured in the *temenos* area probably was used not only to light the oil lamps, but also was sold to worshippers as an "approved" product that could be mixed with their burnt grain offerings.

Temple industries in sacred areas have a long history in Palestine—a fact that gives additional support to the likelihood that the Dan installation was an olive press. In the *temenos* at Nahariyah, Moshe Dothan found a stone mold for casting a metal figurine (probably of silver) in the forecourt of the sanctuary. This mold dates to the Middle Bronze period (c. 1800-1550 B.C.) Apparently, the stone mold was used to manufacture naked horned-goddess figurines in the cultic area, for use in some religious rite.

---

* Stager points out that "virgin oil" was still being used in sanctuary lamps in this century in Artas, a Moslem community near Bethlehem. G. M. Crowfoot and L. Baldensperger, in *From Cedar to Hyssop* (New York, 1932), pp. 28-29, describe the oil manufacturing this way:

"There is a rock face with a shelf in it and there are holes on the floor of the shelf in which the women beat and bruise the olives with a stone pounder. When crushed, the pulp is placed in hot water and the oil skimmed from the top when it rises, and this oil is thought to be very pure and peculiarly suitable for offerings to holy places to be burnt in the lamps hung there."

Newly uncovered, *the central basin of an olive press at Tel Batash still brims with broken storage jars and other debris. Two buried stone vats with plastered stone platforms around their mouths flank the basin. Also discovered near the press, but not seen in this photo, were two large stone weights.*

Olive oil was extracted in this press by the same two-step method proposed for the Tel Dan installation. First, the olives were crushed in the central vat. Then the pulp was loaded into baskets that were stacked directly onto the stone platforms. The pulp was then pressed by a weighted beam, and expressed oil flowed into the vats.

Dothan also discovered seven-spouted oil lamps within the sacred precinct at Nahariyah. The oil for the lamps as well as for offerings may have been produced nearby in a sunken, slate-lined receptacle that was probably an olive crushing vat like the central receptacle at Dan.

At Hazor in the courtyard of the Late Bronze I (1550-1400 B.C.) temple, Yigael Yadin found clear indications of an on-the-spot industry serving temple needs—in this case, a pottery kiln to fire small vessels to contain the offerings of worshippers. The pottery vessels were probably sold to worshippers making offerings at the temple. A similar arrangement was found at Iron Age II (eighth-seventh centuries B.C.) Arad.

In the cultic structure at tenth-century B.C. Ta'anach, evidence of still another type of temple-related on-site industry was discovered, a clay mold for making terra-cotta figurines of the "Tambourine Goddess."

In New Testament times, pigeons, oxen and sheep for sacrifice were sold to worshippers in the court of the Jerusalem Temple (Mark 11:15, John 2:14). The First Temple was also a bustling scene of activity and industry connected with the cult.

Their reinterpretation of the Dan "water libation" installation as an olive press leads Stager and Wolff to take a fresh look at other installations, including one at Tell el-Farah (North), that had also been interpreted as a cult installation. It, too, according to Stager and Wolff, is an olive press. At Farah (North) Roland de Vaux found what he described as a square pedestal base next to a hollowed-out stone basin. (The small stone basin was replaced by a larger slab-lined one in a subsequent rebuilding.) Nearby, protruding through an upper level, de Vaux found a crudely dressed monolith. De Vaux assumed that the monolith was originally erected on the stone pedestal base.

De Vaux imaginatively reconstructed an "open-air shrine" just inside the city gate, complete with *massebah* (the stone monolith) on a pedestal and a basin receptacle for libations.

Stager and Wolff observe, however, that the monolith and slab-lined basin were part of an olive press. "The Farah basin should be interpreted as an olive crushing vat and the *massebah* desacralized to the less exalted status of an olive crusher." Stager and Wolff conclude, "By pouring oil on these lustral waters, we hope to have quieted the stirrings of the water cult."

Before publication of this article, **BAR** asked Biran and Laughlin how they would answer Stager and Wolff's analysis.

Avraham Biran indicated that his conclusions had not changed.

John Laughlin (in a letter to **BAR** dated February 4, 1984) cautions that "there is not yet sufficient archaeological evidence to determine the function of the installation." He adds: "Stager and Wolff have argued quite cogently that the installation is an olive press, and further evidence may prove them right. But until such evidence is forthcoming, it is difficult to accept their interpretation." Laughlin's reasons follow:

"The construction of the installation does not fit that of most known olive presses, which are usually made from solid stone.

"The basin at Dan has an open, unsealed bottom. It is hard to imagine how produce of any sort could have been crushed in it without considerable loss of the liquid. There is no archaeological evidence that the bottom of the basin was ever coated with plaster.

"Stager and Wolff interpret the pile of perforated stones found adjacent to the basin as counterweights for beams used to press the olives. Such an interpretation is possible but certainly not necessary. If the Danites were ever a part of the Sea Peoples, as some have argued, then the stones might indeed have been 'votive anchors.' On the other hand, they may have been used for nothing other than to tether animals. Or again, they may have had no practical or cultic function at all."

Laughlin observes that perhaps the most damaging criticism of Stager and Wolff's interpretation concerns their conclusion that the oil expressed from the pulp on top of the slabs flowed into the jars by way of 'grooves' cut into the slabs. Biran noted in the *Israel Exploration Journal (IEJ)*[4] that a groove or slit was carved in the southern slab in order to facilitate the flow of liquid into the mouth of the jar, and a similar channel was molded in the plaster covering the northern slab. Laughlin's article in **BAR** included an almost identical statement. Laughlin now comments in his letter to **BAR** that "the section [in his **BAR** article] was expanded. . . . This," he says, "has led to a misconception as to the facts of what was actually found . . . which I hope to clear up," as follows:

"Only the southern slab has a 'groove' and not only

Giant olive crusher? *As tall as a grown man, this crudely dressed monolith located near a hollowed out basin, not shown in the photo, at Tel-el Farah (North) has become the subject of a scholarly debate. The excavator, Roland de Vaux, claimed that the monolith was a massebah, or standing stone, in an "open-air shrine." The nearby basin served, said de Vaux, as a receptacle for libations. Other archaeologists, Lawrence Stager and Samuel Wolff, now argue that the monolith was a massive olive pulp crusher, used to force oil from olives that were crushed in the stone basin.*

does it *not* extend the entire length of the slab, it may be nothing other than a natural fissure in the rock. The northern slab *does not contain any kind of groove* and to my knowledge, there is no archaeological evidence to suggest that it was ever coated with plaster. There was certainly none on it when we excavated it. Consequently, there is no evidence that the northern slab ever had any kind of groove or channel in it. Furthermore, there is no collection basin of any kind on either of these slabs, their shape being such that if olives were pressed on them by any means, the oil would easily flow in every

"An olive press"

Stager

Wolff

**BAR readers Terry and Cathy Small
first suggested an olive press.**

direction."[Emphasis J.L.]

Although Biran and Laughlin hold to their view of a water installation at Dan, Stager and Wolff's arguments have convinced most of the scholarly world that it is an oil press. William G. Dever has called their analysis "brilliant."[5]

"A cultic installation"

Biran

Laughlin

But for all the brilliance of Stager and Wolff's analysis, credit for first publication of the idea that oil—not water—was flowing into the sunken vats at Dan must go to **BAR** readers Cathy and Terry Small.—**S.F.S.**

[1] Avraham Biran, "Two Discoveries at Tel Dan," *Israel Exploration Journal (IEJ)* 30 (1980), p. 90.
[2] George L. Kelm and Amihai Mazar, "Notes and News: Tel Batash (Timnah), 1982," *Israel Exploration Journal* 33 (1983), p. 126 and esp. Plate 16:C.
[3] Lawrence E. Stager, "The Finest Olive Oil in Samaria," *Journal of Semitic Studies* XXVIII/1 (Spring 1983).
[4] Biran, *IEJ* 30 (1980), p. 90.
[5] William G. Dever, "Material Remains and the Cult in Ancient Israel: An Essay in Archeological Systematics," *The Word of the Lord Shall Go Forth—Essays in Honor of David Noel Freedman in Celebration of His Sixtieth Birthday*, p. 584, note 30.

CHAPTER FIVE

Archaeology can be complicated, tough and contentious, and so can archaeologists, as seen in the previous chapter. But archaeology can also be beautifully clear: It provides an intimate and immediate connection with people who lived long ago. All who have volunteered on a dig will recall the simple thrill of holding something in their hands that someone else held long ago. Might it have belonged to an ancient queen, a peasant, a royal scribe or a peddler?

Avraham Biran fully appreciates both these aspects of archaeology—the cloudy and the clear, the tough and the easy. In describing this bronze scepter head, which *BAR* designated as the "prize find" of the summer of 1988, he speaks with the simple joy of a first-time volunteer: "We held in our hands ... a scepter that must have been similar to those held by kings and priests in antiquity."

TEL DAN SCEPTER HEAD
Prize Find

AVRAHAM BIRAN

"And it was so, when the king saw Esther the queen standing in the court, that she obtained favor in his sight. And the king held out to Esther the golden scepter that was in his hand. So Esther drew near, and touched the top of the scepter" (Esther 5:2).

AS WE READ in the Book of Esther, the queen was able to approach King Ahasuerus unannounced and, as a result of this audience, Esther eventually saved her people.

The Bible refers to scepters on several occasions as symbols of authority and office (for example, Numbers 24:17; Psalm 45:6; Isaiah 14:5; Zechariah 10:11). The reference in Esther, however, is the only time the top of the scepter is specifically mentioned. What did the "top of the scepter" that Queen Esther touched look like? From the text we have no idea, although we are told that it was made of gold.

The Hebrew Union College-Jewish Institute of Religion has been digging at Tel Dan, in northern Israel, since 1974. Recently we uncovered the top, or head, of a bronze scepter that we believe resembled the gold scepter referred to in the book of Esther.

Dan was the northernmost site in the

©HEBREW UNION COLLEGE/JEWISH INSTITUTE OF RELIGION

Symbol of a king's *or a priest's office, this bronze and silver scepter head was discovered beneath an eighth-century B.C. altar at Tel Dan, the northernmost city in the Biblical kingdom of Israel.*

Four badly corroded figures, possibly representing lion heads, jut from the top of the 3.7-inch-high artifact. Below the figures, three circular grooves form four veins, or rings, a motif that repeats three more times on the scepter head. Around the head's middle section, a bronze ring in the shape of leaves encloses a silver surface. The scepter head terminates at the bottom with an encircling flange.

©HEBREW UNION COLLEGE/JEWISH INSTITUTE OF RELIGION

Biblical kingdom of Israel referred to in the often mentioned Biblical phrase "from Dan to Beer-Sheva." During the last two decades, we have revealed many remarkable finds,* not the least of which is the religious sanctuary located on the northern part of the city near a spring that is of one of the sources of the Jordan River. Here King Jeroboam of the northern kingdom of Israel set up a golden calf as an alternative to the kingdom of Judah's Jerusalem temple (1 Kings 12:26-30). Here we found the bilingual Aramaic and Greek inscription "To the God who is in Dan." Here, too, in a room of a long building we excavated, we found a 3-foot-square altar built of five stones. Nearby three iron shovels or censers used for incense or to remove ashes in a cultic ceremony came to light. Between one of the shovels and the altar lay a jar full of ashes. Analysis of these ashes showed them to be the remains of incense and unidentifiable animal bones.

These finds were described for **BAR** readers in 1987.** Shortly after this article appeared, we decided to remove the stones

* "Danaans and Danites—Were the Hebrews Greek?" **BAR,** June 1982; "Is the Cultic Installation at Dan Really an Olive Press?" **BAR,** Nov./Dec. 1984; "King David as Builder," Mar. 1975; John C.H. Laughlin, "The Remarkable Discoveries at Tel Dan," **BAR,** Sept./Oct. 1981. ** Hershel Shanks, "Avraham Biran—Twenty Years of Digging at Tel Dan," **BAR,** July/August 1987.

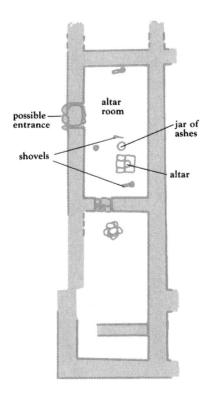

possible entrance

shovels

altar room

jar of ashes

altar

0   5m

Who would guess *that this three-by-three-foot stone altar (above) concealed a remarkable artifact? Yet when dig director Avraham Biran had the altar dismantled (opposite, above), he discovered a unique head of a scepter concealed beneath it. The altar stood in a room the excavators now refer to as the "altar room" (see plan, left), adjacent to the lishkah, or chamber, where priests may have officiated; this structure was apparently an eighth-century B.C. addition to the religious sanctuary at Tel Dan. The upper half of a jar found upside down in the hole above the altar contained the ashes of burned incense and unidentifiable animal bones. Three iron shovels (opposite, below), probably used during religious rites, were also found next to the altar, as shown in the plan. The earliest of their kind ever found, these shovels resemble incense shovels pictured on synagogue mosaic floors of the fourth to fifth centuries A.D.*

of the altar in order to exhibit them in Jerusalem in our Skirball Museum for Biblical Archaeology. Naturally, we also wanted to see if there was anything beneath the altar. Beneath the stones of the altar we discovered a unique object: the head of a scepter!

The scepter head is 3.7 inches high and 1.5 inches in diameter. Made of bronze and hollow in the center, it weighs a little less than a pound—14 ounces to be exact.

Around the central part of the scepter

With scepter upraised, *a goddess sits on her throne in this scene impressed in damp clay by rolling an inscribed Akkadian cylinder seal across it. A worshipper, carrying a kid, faces the goddess and pours a libation over a flaming altar. The seal with its goddess, dating to about 2360-2180 B.C., differs from most examples of scepters on ancient seals and in ancient texts, where they are shown with human rulers.*

head a ring of bronze in the shape of leaves encloses a silver surface. Four badly corroded protrusions on top have been identified as lion heads. Below the lion heads three circular grooves form four veins, or rings, a motif that appears three more times on the scepter head. A flange encircles the bottom of the scepter head.

You can imagine the excitement not only of the students, but of the staff as well, at making such a find. We held in our hands the head, or top, of a scepter that must have been similar to those held by kings and priests in antiquity. It was then that we thought that our scepter might well resemble the top of the scepter Queen Esther had touched, although ours is made of bronze, not gold, and dates to the ninth

century B.C.E.,* a few centuries before the Esther story.

Scepter heads have been found in a number of excavations. In some of the older excavations, they were misinterpreted as feet of furniture. Some especially significant scepter tops were discovered by Henry Layard in 1850 in the northwest palace of Nimrud in Mesopotamia. These scepter tops were also made of bronze, sometimes inlaid with iron. Inscribed names appeared on four of them.[1]

It is possible that a name—or something else—is inscribed on our scepter head. We

---

* B.C.E. is the scholarly, religiously neutral designation equivalent to B.C. It stands for "before the common era."

will know for sure only after experts remove the corrosion on the scepter head and complete their laboratory analysis.

Scepters appear most commonly in ancient texts and glyptic art as symbols of earthly rulers, but in at least one case a cylinder seal displays a scepter in the hand of a goddess.[2] Because our scepter head was found beneath an altar we can speculate that it may have belonged to a priest at Dan. Perhaps future finds will substantiate this conjecture.

[1] See R.D. Barnett in *Eretz Israel*, vol. 8 (Jerusalem, 1967), p. 4ff.
[2] James A. Pritchard, *The Ancient Near East in Pictures* (Princeton, NJ: Princeton Univ. Press, 1954), p. 222.

CHAPTER SIX

July 21, 1993. On that date the field of Biblical archaeology utterly changed. A large broken slab of basalt was found at Dan. The lengthy Aramaic inscription scratched with a metal tool into one face contained two phrases that thrilled the world: "House of David" and "King of Israel." Dating to the ninth century B.C., the inscription is the earliest extra-Biblical reference to David or his dynasty. In this photo of Biran, taken soon after the discovery, the archaeologist openly grins as he sits at a laboratory table laden with his plans, books, clay artifacts and magnifying glass—and his "House of David" inscription.

A few months later, Biran would find two more fragments of the inscription.

I t's not often that an archaeological find makes the front page of the *New York Times* (to say nothing of *Time* magazine). But that is what happened last summer to a discovery at Tel Dan, a beautiful mound in northern Galilee, at the foot of Mt. Hermon beside one of the headwaters of the Jordan River.[1]

There Avraham Biran and his team of archaeologists[2] found a remarkable inscription from the ninth century B.C.E. that refers both to the "House of David" and to the "King of Israel." This is the first time that the name David has been found in any ancient inscription outside the Bible. That the inscription refers not simply to a "David" but to the House of David, the dynasty of the great Israelite king, is even more remarkable.

Inscription crowns 27 years of exciting discoveries.

"King of Israel" is a term frequently found in the Bible, especially in the Book of Kings. This, however, may be the oldest extra-Biblical reference to Israel in Semitic script. If this inscription proves anything, it shows that both Israel and Judah, contrary to the claims of some scholarly Biblical minimizers, were important kingdoms at this time.

Together with his colleague Professor Joseph Naveh of the Hebrew University, Professor Biran promptly wrote a scientific report on the inscription, which was published in the *Israel Exploration Journal*.[3] This special article for **BAR** readers is based on that report and on other materials supplied by Professor Biran.

"DAVID" FOUND

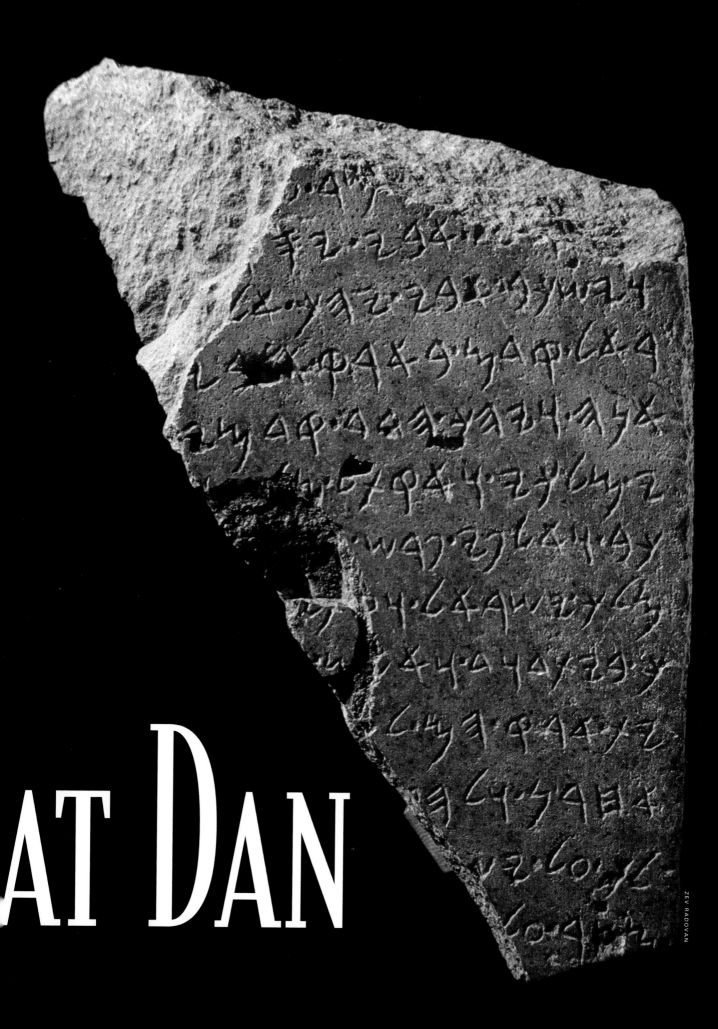

AT DAN

"OF THE BUTCHERS" says the Aramaic inscription on the 4-inch-wide base of this pottery bowl. Incised after the bowl was fired, the ninth-century B.C.E. inscription suggests that the bowl belonged to the butchers or cooks of the royal household at Dan. The bowl was found by accident on the surface of the mound the year before excavation began. The drawing shows the inscription, with dashed lines indicating reconstructed portions.

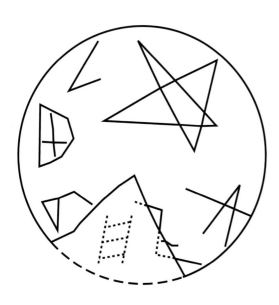

Let us start with some background. In the first season at Tel Dan—27 years ago, in 1966—Biran and his team uncovered on the slope of the mound a small potsherd incised with four letters in ancient Hebrew script (see photo, p. 78). Although inscriptions are quite rare in excavations in Israel, the excavators were not really surprised. In the previous year, a ninth-century B.C.E. Aramaic inscription incised on the base of a bowl had been discovered quite by accident on the surface of the site. The late Professor Nahman Avigad, who published the inscription, read it as "of the butchers." The bowl on which it was inscribed had probably belonged to the cooks or butchers in the royal household of Dan.[4]

The four-letter Hebrew inscription on the potsherd was dated to the eighth century B.C.E., about a century after the "butcher" inscription. The four letters read l'mṣ (לאמץ). The first letter is the common preposition meaning "belonging to"; the last three letters are a name: Amotz. This was the name of the father of the prophet Isaiah (Isaiah 1:1; 2 Kings 19:2; 2 Chronicles 26:22, etc.), who prophesied in the eighth century B.C.E. The jar did not belong to Isaiah's father—the name was fairly common—but the discovery of an eighth-century B.C.E. inscription with a well-known name naturally caused considerable excitement for the members of the expedition and raised hopes of finding more.

Two years later, in 1968, while excavating a seventh-century B.C.E. building, Biran found a sherd inscribed with seven letters in Phoenician script (see photo, p. 78). It read lb'lplṭ (לבעלפלט), meaning "belonging to Baalpelet." The name Baalpelet means "may Baal rescue." As Baal was a pagan god, it is unlikely that Baalpelet the jar owner was an Israelite.

We have no idea who this Baalpelet was. Twenty years later, however, on the northern part of the mound, Biran found another ostracon inscribed with the letters l and ṭ, probably the last letters of the same name (see photo, p. 78). Baalpelet may have been a prominent member of the Dan community, if having two jars inscribed with his name is any indication. Alternatively, the name may simply have been popular in the seventh century B.C.E.

Eight years later, in 1976, in a disturbed level of occupation (thus, it cannot be precisely dated by stratigraphy), the Tel Dan team found an unusual bilingual inscription—in Greek and Aramaic—incised on a stone, mentioning the "God who is in Dan." This inscription conclusively established that the site was Biblical Dan (see photo, p. 79).

Another ten excavation seasons passed without a hint of an inscription. Then, in 1986, in a layer of violent destruction attributed to the Assyrian conquest of northern Israel by Tiglath-pileser III in 733/732 B.C.E., a

THE TEL DAN EXCAVATION, seen in the foreground, began in 1966. Israel's longest ongoing dig, Tel Dan continues to produce remarkable discoveries. In the upper left, the foothills of Mt. Hermon rise from the cultivated plain.

Yahwistic name that may reflect Immadiyo's, or his parents', devotion to the Israelite God.

In 1988, they uncovered another Yahwistic name on an eighth-century B.C.E. jar handle: *zkryo* (זכריו), meaning "God (Yahweh) remembers" or "May God (Yahweh) remember" (see photo, p. 80). This is a very common name in the Bible, perhaps more easily recognizable by transliterating it with vowels: Zecharya or, even more recognizably, Zechariah or Zachariah (the same name in Hebrew). Another Biblical form of the name is Zecharyahu, especially in Judah. Young's Bible concordance lists 27 different men named Zechariah in the Bible, and two named Zachariah. In the New Testament, Zechariah was the name of John the Baptist's father (Luke 1).

One of the Biblical Zechariahs was the son of Jeroboam II; he succeeded his father to the throne of Israel (in about 753 B.C.E.) and held it for a bare six months. At that time Dan was included in the kingdom of Israel. It is tantalizing to imagine that perhaps the seal belonged to a king, King Zechariah of eighth-century B.C.E. Israel. The date of the seal impression and the date of the king's reign do seem to fit.

In addition to these inscriptions, the Tel Dan team made many other important discoveries: the unique triple-arched gate, the Mycenaean tomb, the scepter head and the Israelite gate complex.** None was more

stamped jar handle was found (see photo, p. 32), bearing the letters *l'mdyo* (לעמדיו). The seal that made the impression had belonged to someone named *Immadiyo*, that is, "God is with me." The *-yo* (יו) element in the name is a shortened form of Yahweh (the personal name of the Israelite God) used in the northern kingdom, Israel.* Immadiyo is thus a

* The shortened form of Yahweh used in names in the southern kingdom, Judah, was *-yahu*.

UNUSUALLY LARGE Phoenician script, deeply incised before firing of the original vessel, forms the inscription on the potsherd at right. The inscription reads, "belonging to Baalpelet" (*lb'lplṭ*). The name means "may Baal rescue," referring to the pagan god Baal, so it may not belong to an Israelite. Excavated from a seventh-century B.C.E. building in 1968, the ostracon, or inscribed potsherd, measures about 10 inches wide and 9 inches high.

Another ostracon (left) with the letters *l* and *ṭ* together, probably the end of the same name, turned up 20 years later in the northern part of the mound. Whether this ostracon and sherd both refer to the same person, or whether it was simply a popular name remains unknown.

** For the gates and tomb, see John C.H. Laughlin, "The Remarkable Discoveries at Tel Dan," **BAR**, September/October 1981; for the scepter head, see Avraham Biran, "Tel Dan Scepter Head," **BAR**, January/February 1989. Also see Hershel Shanks, "Avraham Biran—Twenty Years of Digging at Tel Dan," **BAR**, July/August 1987.

DEFINITELY DAN. Professor Biran's 1976 discovery of this 6-by-10-inch limestone tablet confirmed the identity of the site he was digging. The bilingual inscription in Greek (top three lines) and Aramaic (bottom line) refers to a person named Zoilos who made a vow to the "god who is in Dan," or, in an alternative reading, to the "god of the Danites." Found in Tel Dan's sacred area, this votive inscription dates to the late third or early second centuries B.C. based on the style of the scripts.

dramatic, however, than the inscription uncovered last summer referring to the "House of David" and the "King of Israel."

In a sense the find can be attributed to the fact that the Israel Government Tourist Corporation and the Antiquities Authority had decided that Tel Dan was a site worthy of a major conservation and restoration project, so that, after nearly a generation of excavation, the site can be properly presented to visitors. As part of this project, which began in 1992, the archaeologists removed the debris from the eighth-century B.C.E. Assyrian destruction level—the destruction of Tiglath-pileser III, as previously mentioned—outside the city-gate complex. The purpose was simply to remove this destruction debris. But, as so often happens in an excavation, the unexpected occurred. As the destruction debris was being removed, an intriguing new ninth-century B.C.E. gate was uncovered; it formed an additional outer gate leading to the city-gate complex.

The previously known city-gate complex consisted of an outer gate that opened into a rectangular pavement (about 28 feet long and 65 feet wide), on the other side of which stood the major, or inner, gate. In this

plaza, just as one approached the inner gate, a low platform had been uncovered several years ago (see photo, p. 82). It had sockets at three of the four corners (the fourth socket was missing) that apparently once supported a canopy over the platform. The platform was probably either for the city's ruler, to greet a parade of dignitaries along a beautifully paved processional route, or a pedestal for the statue of a deity. To the right was a bench where perhaps the elders sat—to judge cases, to make deals or to welcome a royal procession.

In 1992, as part of the conservation-preservation project, Biran made an unexpected find when the layer of destruction in this area was removed. A decorated capital that may have adorned the top of one of the columns of the canopied structure above the platform was excavated (see photo, p. 83).

The next surprising find was a set of five standing stones in a niche just inside the outer gate (see photo, p. 83). At either end of this row of standing stones lay large, carefully hewn, rectangular blocks. These blocks apparently belonged originally to part of the structure that sheltered the standing stones. The nature of these stones and their location—along the city wall in the plaza of the city-gate complex—together with a cache of some 25 pottery vessels found west of the standing stones, suggests that they may be sacred pillars, the *massebot* often mentioned in the Bible. This suggestion is further buttressed by the votive nature of

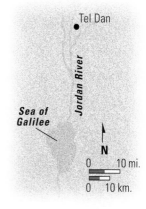

Stamped Jar Handles Provide More Inscriptions

Jar handles stamped with the owner's name have turned up several times in the Dan excavation. The destruction layer attributed to the conquest of northern Israel in 733/732 B.C.E. by the Assyrian king Tiglath-pileser III yielded such an inscription in 1986 (top and left-hand drawing). The paleo-Hebrew script reads *l'mdyo* (belonging to Immadiyo). The name means "God is with me." The element *yo* or *yau* was the form used in the northern kingdom of Israel for Yahweh, the Israelite God.

Another eighth-century B.C.E. example (bottom and right-hand drawing), found in 1988, bears the name *zkryo* in paleo-Hebrew script. Transliterated with vowels, this spells Zechariah or Zachariah (meaning "God [Yahweh] remembers" or "May God [Yahweh] remember"). Twenty-seven people in the Bible have this name, and one of them is King Zechariah of Israel, who reigned for six months in about 753 B.C.E. It is tantalizing to think that the jar may have been royal property, but this must remain in the realm of conjecture.

the vessels: nine oil lamps, three of which have a pedestal and seven spouts; five three-legged cups (possibly for incense); four flat and five deep bowls; and numerous other stands. All of these artifacts are known to have cultic functions.

In short, this evidence suggests that the plaza between the outer and inner gates had a small "gateway" sanctuary that could be considered a *bamah* (often translated "high place") of the kind mentioned in 2 Kings 23:1-20. That Biblical passage describes the seventh-century religious reforms instituted by King Josiah. Like King Hezekiah before him, Josiah wanted to centralize all worship of the Israelite God Yahweh in the Jerusalem Temple. To ensure this, Josiah destroyed the outlying *bamot* (plural of *bamah*). In this connection, the Biblical text specifically mentions "*bamot* of the gates" and one that was at the "entrance" (*petach*) of a gate (2 Kings 23:8). The *bamah* at Dan may have been this kind of structure.

In 1993, Biran and his team continued clearing the area outside the outer gate of the city-gate complex, because they knew that the paved plaza extended there, both to the east and to the south. There they uncovered approximately 475 square yards of pavement outside the outer city gate. Then on the east they hit a wall that had undergone considerable change, including the construction of a water channel through it in the Roman period. On the northern side of this wall, they found the "House of David/King of Israel" inscription, but that is getting ahead of the story.

South of this plaza outside the city-gate complex was a row of five unworked stones (one was missing). On either side of this row of stones lay a squared stone, on top of which was a stone pivot set inside the door socket. It seemed that they had discovered another gate, still farther out from the other one, and that this was its threshold (see box, pp. 84-85). The two hemispherical stone pivots, made of local black basalt, once held square wooden doorposts, as reflected in the square hole in each of them. Thus the doors resting on the hemispherical pivots could be opened and closed with ease. The function of this new outer gate—an outer outer gate—is still unclear.

The biggest surprise was, of course, the inscription. The team's surveyor, Gila Cook, first noticed it. There, in secondary use *in* a wall, on the east side of the plaza, beneath an eighth-century B.C.E. destruction level, she saw a basalt stone protruding from the ground. As the rays of the afternoon sun glanced off this stone, Gila thought she saw letters on it and called Biran over. When he bent down to look at the stone, he exclaimed: "Oh, my God, we have an inscription!" The stone was easily removed and, when turned toward the sun, the letters sprang to life. In their words, "It was an unforgettable moment."

The piece of basalt was a fragment of what must have been a large monumental inscription. The box

A CHARIOTEER adorns this beautifully preserved krater, one of several Late Bronze Age Mycenaean imports found in a well-built tomb at Dan. Other funerary offerings included gold and silver jewelry, bronze swords and ivory cosmetic boxes. The tomb and its contents date to the heyday of Canaanite Laish in the 14th or 13th century B.C.E. and testify to the city's prosperity and extensive trade relations before its conquest by the Israelite tribe of Dan (Joshua 19:47; Judges 18:29).

on pages 86-87 contains a drawing of the 13-line inscription, a transcript in modern Hebrew letters and an English translation. In the translation, the words and letters in brackets have been reconstructed on the basis of surviving parts of the inscription. A dot over a letter in the modern Hebrew transcription indicates that the letter has only partially survived.

Parts of 13 lines have been preserved, but not a single one is complete. In the first line, only three letters have survived. In the second line are five letters and part of a sixth; in the last line, only five letters; and the widest line has a mere 14 letters.

On the other hand, the surviving letters are clearly engraved and easy to read. The script is in Old Hebrew letters, sometimes called paleo-Hebrew, the kind of letters used before the Babylonian destruction of the First Temple in 586 B.C.E. When the Jews returned from the Babylonian exile, they brought back the square Aramaic script still used today.

Dots separate the words, as was then customary. In line 9, where "House of David" appears, however, the two Hebrew words *bytdwd* are not separated by a dot,

A LABYRINTHINE GATE COMPLEX confronted the ancient visitor who wished to enter the Israelite city of Dan in the First Temple period, as shown in this isometric reconstruction (right). After entering via the recently discovered outer outer gate and paved plaza (see p. 84), the visitor would pass through the outer gate into a small plaza containing five standing stones constituting a shrine (opposite) and a low platform of hewn limestone blocks covered by a canopy, which may have served as a throne or held a cult statue (below).

Round, carved, socketed bases—two beside the platform on the left and one on the right—indicate that posts were inserted into the holes to support the canopy over the platform. A presumed fourth base has disappeared. This platform may perhaps be explained by, and in turn illustrate, a passage in the Bible: "Then the king arose and took his seat in the gate...and all the people came before the king" (2 Samuel 19:8). To the right of the platform, a stone bench, perhaps for the elders of the city, lines the wall for about 16 feet.

Next the visitor would pass through the four-chambered inner gate, which measures almost 100 feet wide and 60 feet through its passage and dates to the ninth century B.C.E. The two rooms on each side of the entryway probably housed the guards.

Continuing to follow the pavement, the visitor would come at last to the 55-by-40-foot upper gate, beyond which lay the city itself.

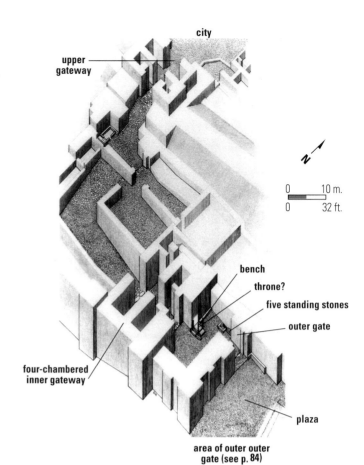

city

upper gateway

N

0   10 m.
0   32 ft.

bench

throne?

five standing stones

outer gate

four-chambered inner gateway

plaza

area of outer outer gate (see p. 84)

DROOPING LEAVES, a motif well known from Assyrian ivories, decorate this foot-high limestone capital found in 1992. Another decorative element appears above the leaves. The capital may have adorned the top of a column supporting the canopied structure that protected the low platform between the outer and inner gates.

but written together, like HouseofDavid. The dynastic name of the kingdom of Judah, whose founder was King David, was apparently regarded as one word.

Note that the first letter (farthest to the right) in line 9, just before the reference to the House of David, is the last letter of *melech*, the Hebrew word for king, so the previous line probably ended with the other two letters of the word for king. In short, there was probably a reference to "the king of the House of David." Perhaps the missing part even gave his name.

In line 8 is a reference to *melech yisrael*, the king of Israel, so the text mentions both the northern kingdom of Israel and the southern kingdom of Judah and the king of each. Unfortunately, the kings' names, if they were ever there, have not survived.

In line 5, however, is the name Hadad. Hadad was a storm god, especially popular among the Arameans east of the Jordan. "Hadad went in front of me," the text reads. This is apparently a victory stela erected in Dan by an Aramean king devoted to Hadad.

Line 4 reads: "...rael formerly in my father's land." Apparently the two letters that were at the end of line 3 were "Is" so that the original text read "Israel formerly in my father's land." There may even have been a reference to the cities of Israel.

In lines 6 and 7, the author of the text boasts that he "slew [some apparently large number of] chariots and 2,000 horsemen." Then the following lines con-

tain references to the king of Israel and, presumably, the king of the House of David.

Thus this appears to be a victory stela erected in Dan by an Aramean, a devotee of Hadad, who is boasting of his military victory over Israel and perhaps also Judah. That this is an Aramean victory stela is confirmed by the fact that the language is Early Aramaic, related to, but slightly different from, Hebrew. The author of the text was probably not the Aramean king, but rather a military commander of the king's, because in line 6 we find a reference to "my king." On the other hand, lines 2 and 3 refer to "my father" and line 4 refers to "my father's land," indicating royalty of some sort. Perhaps the military commander who erected the stela was him-

FIVE SMALL STONES, perhaps Biblical *massebot*, stand in a niche against the city wall, just inside the outer gate (see plan, p. 84). Large, well-hewn, rectangular blocks flank the standing stones, indicating that a structure may have sheltered the stones. The discovery of some 25 votive pottery vessels nearby supports the idea of a cultic function for these stones.

self a royal personage, possibly a king who was subordinate to the king of Aram who ruled from Damascus. The Bible actually mentions two such subordinate kingdoms, Maacah (2 Samuel 10:6,8; 1 Chronicles 19:7) and Rehob (Samuel 10:8). Although Maacah and Rehob were more than a hundred years before the Dan stela was written, these kingdoms may still have existed in the period of the stela.

In 1 Kings 15:16-22 (a parallel account appears in 2 Chronicles 16:1-6), we learn of a war between King Baasha of Israel and King Asa of Judah. Asa took all the gold and silver from the Jerusalem Temple and from his own palace and presented it to Ben-Hadad, king of Aram, as a gift, with a note requesting Ben-Hadad's help. Ben-Hadad responded by attacking cities in the northern kingdom of Israel, and captured several of them, *including Dan* (1 Kings 15:20).

Does this Biblical episode provide the historical background of the Dan stela? Did Ben-Hadad, the Aramean, erect this victory stela after capturing Dan?

The answer depends on (1) whether the date of the stela is contemporaneous with this episode, and (2) whether the two texts "fit" with one another.

The Biblical episode can be dated to the first half of the ninth century B.C.E., about 885. (Baasha's reign extended from 906 to 883 and Asa's reign from 908 to 867.)

How was the stela dated to the ninth century B.C.E.? One way to date the inscription is paleographically—by the shape and stance of the letters. On this basis, Joseph Naveh dated the inscription to the ninth century. The evidence comes from other inscriptions that have been previously dated. In the ninth century, Aramaic script and Phoenician script had not yet gone their separate ways, so comparisons to inscriptions in both scripts are relevant. Unfortunately, however, most extant ninth-century inscriptions, like the famous Mesha stela, which is most similar to the Dan inscription, come from the latter half of that century. Only the Phoenician Nora inscription* and an inscription from Cyprus come from the early ninth century. So, the Dan inscription can be dated paleographically to about the middle of the century, but might fall within a range of some decades earlier or later.

An archaeological analysis, however, suggests a date in the first half of the ninth century. The stela fragment that bears the inscription was used in a wall that was destroyed by Tiglath-pileser III in 733/732 B.C.E., so the stela must have been erected before this date. But that doesn't help much.

The pottery from the level beneath the stela fragment narrows the range. While the amount of pottery found there was small, none of it was later than the first half of the ninth century! This suggests that the

---

*See Joan G. Scheuer, "Searching for the Phoenicians in Sardinia," **BAR**, January/February 1990; and Edward Lipinski, "Epigraphy in Crisis—Dating Ancient Semitic Inscriptions," **BAR**, July/August 1990.

Destruction Debris Yields Plaza, New Gate and Inscription

The clearance of destruction debris from the conquest of Dan by Assyrian king Tiglath-pileser III in 733/732 B.C.E. brought forth a wealth of new discoveries in 1992 and 1993. The plan (below) shows the relationship of a newly cleared plaza and a hitherto undiscovered outer outer gate to the previously known outer and inner gates. It also marks the findspot of the "House of David" inscription.

In the upper photo, the newly clearly plaza, measuring 475 square yards and paved with stones, lies in front of the outer gate, at lower right. In the southeast corner of the plaza (lower photo), four unworked stones and one missing stone mark the threshold of the new outer outer gate. This threshold also appears in the upper photo at the edge of the paved plaza, at center, to the left of the man. At each end of this threshold, a large recumbent stone with a socket holds a hemispherical stone pivot made of black basalt. Wooden doorposts once fitted into the square holes in the pivots, allowing the gate doors to swing easily open and closed.

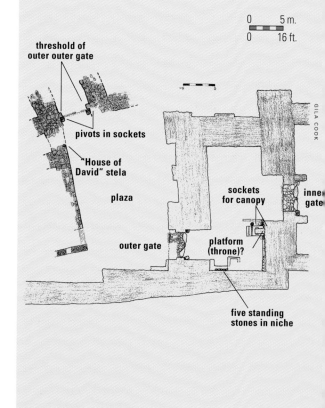

threshold of outer outer gate

pivots in sockets

"House of David" stela

plaza

outer gate

sockets for canopy

platform (throne)?

inner gate

five standing stones in niche

0   5 m.
0   16 ft.

GILA COOK

New Inscription May Illuminate Biblical Events

Tel Dan surveyor Gila Cook first spotted the "House of David" inscription in the glancing rays of the afternoon sun. She called over excavation director Avraham Biran, who, when he saw it, exclaimed, "Oh, my God, we have an inscription!" The photos show the fragmentary stela as it was found (below) and shortly after removal (opposite).

Broken in antiquity and reused as building material, the stela lay in a wall beneath the eighth-century B.C.E. destruction debris from Tiglath-pileser III's conquest (see the plan, page 84). The inscription's 13 partially preserved lines in the Early Aramaic language, written in paleo-Hebrew script of the ninth century B.C.E., uses dots to separate the words (drawing, opposite). Based on associated pottery fragments and evidence from the inscription itself, Professor Biran suggests the stela was erected in the first half of the ninth century B.C.E. Biran and his colleagues continue to search for additional fragments of the stela.

In the translation, the material in brackets represents suggested reconstructions. Fortunately, the phrases "House of David" (the dynastic name of the kingdom of Judah) and "king of Israel" (often used without a specific name in the Books of Kings) need no reconstruction. The inscription seems to commemorate the victory of an Aramean king over the kingdoms of Israel and Judah. One of the Aramean king's military commanders probably erected the stela, for it speaks of "my king" (line 6). In view of the date and the location in Galilee, among other factors, the stela may describe events in the war of Ben Hadad I against King Baasha of Israel in 885 B.C.E. (1 Kings 15:16-22; 2 Chronicles 16:1-6). In any case, it shows that Israel and Judah were important kingdoms in the ninth century B.C.E. When the Israelites reconquered Dan, they apparently destroyed the stela and used its pieces in the wall.

Transcription

[	[מר.ע]]
[	[.אבי.יסק].]
[יש.	וישכב.אבי.יהך.אל].
[	ראל.קדם.בארק.אבי].
[	אנה.ויהך.הדד.קדמי].
[ר.	י.מלכי.ואקתל.מנ]הם.
[	כב.ואלפי.פרש].
[מל].	מלך.ישראל.וקתלת.
[א.	ד.ביתדוד.ואשם].
[	ית.ארק.הם.ל]
[מ.	אחרן.ולה]
[	לך.על.יש[ר]אל.
[	מצר.על].

Translation

(1) ...

(2) ...my father went up

(3) ...and my father died, he went to [his fate...Is-]

(4) rael formerly in my father's land...

(5) I [fought against Israel?] and Hadad went in front of me...

(6) ...my king. And I slew of [them X footmen, Y cha-]

(7) riots and two thousand horsemen...

(8) the king of Israel. And [I] slew [...the kin-]

(9) g of the House of David. And I put...

(10) their land...

(11) other...[...ru-]

(12) led over Is[rael...]

(13) siege upon...

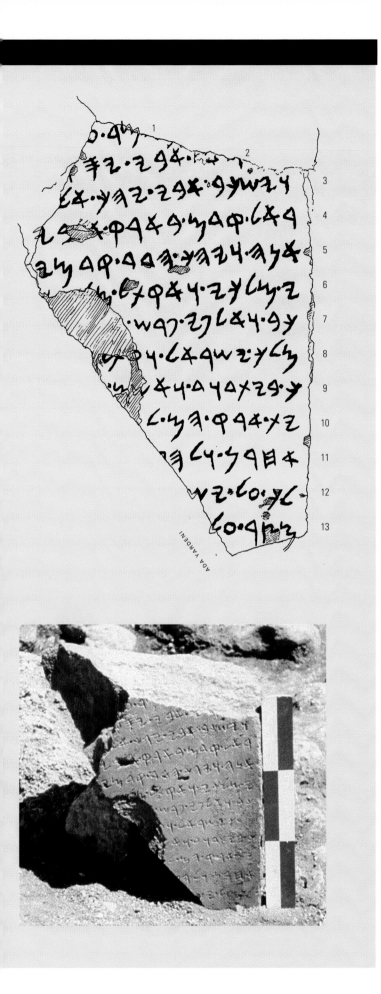

ADA YARDENI

stela was broken up around that time, so that it would have been erected sometime during the first half of the ninth century B.C.E. It must have stood at least some time before being destroyed and used secondarily in the wall. A date early in the ninth century fits nicely with the date of the Biblical episode (about 885 B.C.E.).

But an examination of the two accounts—the one in the Bible and the other on the fragmentary inscription—suggests caution. Obviously, the reconstruction of the text presents many difficulties and many possibilities. Note that in line 9, Naveh and Biran have reconstructed an "I" before "slew," so that the author of the text does the slaying. That is their best guess, although other reconstructions are possible. If the reconstruction of "I" is correct, it appears that the author of the victory stela is claiming a victory over Judah (the House of David), who is his enemy, as well as over Israel. If that is so, it would conflict with the Biblical episode, in which the Aramean king was allied with the king of Judah, having been bribed with a gift of gold and silver. Thus the stela may be describing some other military engagement in which both Judah and Israel were allied against Aram.

There were probably several battles or wars in the ninth century B.C.E. between Aram and Israel. Not all were recorded in the Bible. Indeed, several other possibilities are mentioned in the Bible.[5] For the time being, the matter must remain in the realm of learned conjecture.

In any event, at some point Israel must have regained control of Dan, perhaps when King Ahab rebuilt the city after its destruction by Ben-Hadad I in 885 B.C.E. When the Israelites regained control of the city, the Aramean victory stela was destroyed. The only thing we can be sure of is that it was broken and that one of the fragments was used in a wall bordering a plaza in the city-gate complex.

As stated earlier, this is now the oldest extant Semitic reference to Israel. The "king of Israel" is also referred to in the famous Mesha stela, which, according to most experts, dates later in the ninth century. The immensely important Merneptah stela, dated to 1207 B.C.E., also refers to Israel, but the text is in hieroglyphics. The Tel Dan inscription is therefore the oldest appearance in Semitic script of the name Israel—at least for now. Who knows when a new inscription that challenges this claim will be found.

Photos are courtesy of Avraham Biran and Hebrew Union College–Jewish Institute of Religion.

[1]See the following **BAR** articles: Avraham Biran, "Tel Dan Scepter Head," January/February 1989; Hershel Shanks, "Avraham Biran— Twenty Years of Digging at Tel Dan," July/August 1987; John C.H. Laughlin, "The Remarkable Discoveries at Tel Dan," September/October 1981.
[2]From the Nelson Glueck School of Biblical Archaeology of the Hebrew Union College–Jewish Institute of Religion.
[3]Avraham Biran and Joseph Naveh, "An Aramaic Stele Fragment from Tel Dan," *Israel Exploration Journal* 43 (1993), pp. 81-98.
[4]See *Palestine Exploration Quarterly* 100 (1968), pp. 42-44.
[5]For a discussion, see Biran and Naveh, "An Aramaic Stele Fragment," pp. 95-98.

MORE FRAGMENTS FROM "DAVID" STELA FOUND AT DAN

ZEV RADOVAN

In the summer of 1994, just months after the preceding article appeared in **BAR***, Avraham Biran sent us the following fax directly from the field:*

Last summer a startling inscription was found at Tel Dan that mentioned the "House of David" and "King of Israel." This season, two additional fragments of the stela have been recovered. (All three pieces of the inscription are shown in the photograph, opposite.)

In these two fragments are the name of the Aramean god Hadad, as well as a reference to a battle between the Israelites and the Arameans.

One of the new fragments was found on June 21, almost a year to the day after the main fragment was discovered. It was found about 50 feet northeast of the earlier fragment, on top of debris covering the pavement. When our Druze worker Nabil was removing the excavated material into the wheelbarrow, area supervisor Malka Hershkovitz noticed writing on the basalt stone.

The second new fragment was found by Gila Cook (who also found the main fragment last year) when she was setting a measuring rod into the ground. This new fragment had been used in the pavement that reaches the bottom of the Israelite city wall, built in the mid-ninth century B.C.E.

This pavement along the city wall extends farther east, and there we discovered five more standing stones, *mazzeboth*. These newly uncovered five *mazzeboth* are similar to those already found last year and described in the March/April 1994 **BAR**.

Between the two groups of *mazzeboth*, a *bama* was uncovered with three *mazzeboth* of different sizes, the largest over 3 feet high. A basalt bowl on top of a decorated pedestal lay in front of the largest or main *mazzebah*. The basalt bowl showed signs of fire; the ashes within the entire area indicate that offerings were made here.

It appears that the cult activities at the entrance to Dan and between the city gates were quite elaborate during the 9th and 8th centuries.

Warm regards and *Shabbat Shalom*.

Avraham Biran
Tel Dan
Summer 1994

CHAPTER SEVEN

"Deep in your heart, you always think, 'Wouldn't it be wonderful to find the golden calf.'" Biran didn't find the golden idol erected at Dan by King Jeroboam I of Israel (1 Kings 12:28), but he did uncover evidence of intense cultic activity, including these rusty iron incense shovels (opposite), called *machtot* in the Bible (Leviticus 10:1), and an extraordinary number of sacred standing stones pictured on the following pages. Perhaps as much as the golden calf, these cultic objects bring to life the religious practices of the ancient Israelites at Dan.

SACRED

AVRAHAM BIRAN

Upon King Solomon's death, his kingdom split in two—the kingdom of Judah in the south and that of Israel in the north. A scion of David continued to sit on the Judahite throne in Jerusalem for more than 300 years—until the Babylonian conquest in 586 B.C.E. The north, however, witnessed a succession of rulers from a variety of dynasties. The first king in the north was Jeroboam, who had earlier been a subversive in Solomon's court (1 Kings 11:26-39). When Solomon tried to kill him, the rebellious Jeroboam fled to Egypt (1 Kings 11:40). After Solomon's death, Jeroboam returned and was proclaimed king of secessionist Israel.

But the new king of Israel feared that his people would still want to offer sacrifices at the Jerusalem Temple and might revert to the rule of the Davidic dynasty (1 Kings 12:26,27). To keep his people's allegiances, Jeroboam established two shrines at opposite ends of his kingdom—one at Bethel, in the south, and the other at Dan, in the north. He set up two golden calves, one at Bethel and the other at Dan, for his people to worship. "This is your god, O Israel," he declared (1 Kings 12:28).

Although we have not discovered the golden calf that Jeroboam is said to have set up at Dan, we have probably found the remains of the royal shrine where the calf once stood, built in the late tenth century B.C.E. These remains include a large platform, about 60 feet wide, made of large blocks of stones; this structure, we believe, is an example of an open-air shrine known in the Bible as a *bamah*, often translated as "high place" (in Leviticus 26:30 and in 89 other passages). We also found a number of cult

Of Standing Stones, High Places

SPACES

and Cult Objects at Tel Dan

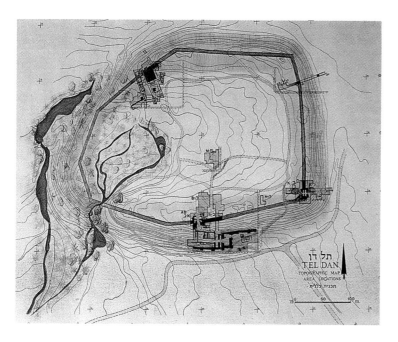

PRECEDING PAGES: Located near the source of the Jordan River and the foothills of Mt. Hermon (shown in the distance), Tel Dan towers some 60 feet above the surrounding plain. Author Avraham Biran has been digging at Dan since 1966—the longest-running excavation in Israel. His efforts have yielded a large array of Israelite cultic sites and ritual artifacts.

After the death of King Solomon, Jeroboam, the newly proclaimed king of Israel, set up a shrine at Dan that housed a golden calf; the king announced to his people: "This is your god, O Israel" (1 Kings 12:28). Biran has found, not one, but several open-air shrines at Dan, including a large stone platform identified as a *bamah*, or high place—where, Biran believes, Jeroboam set up the golden calf. Near this *bamah* were a number of finds associated with cult practices, such as an incense stand, clay figurines and seven-wick oil lamps, one of which is shown on p. 93. A plan of the entire excavation site is shown above. The *bamah* appears in the upper left part of the drawing. The city wall and gate, as well as several sets of *maṣṣebot*, or sacred pillars, appear at the bottom.

objects associated with the shrine, including oil lamps with seven wicks, *pithoi* (large containers) decorated with depictions of snakes, an incense stand, a bowl full of animal bones, figurines of clay and faience, and a sunken basin with slanting basalt slabs. In ancient Israel, the snake was associated with cult practices, particularly with the worship of Baal. Not until King Hezekiah's time (the late eighth century B.C.E.) was Moses' bronze serpent (to which the people of Israel made offerings) ultimately destroyed—along with the *bamot* (high places) and *maṣṣebot* (sacred pillars) (2 Kings 18:4). The basin with slanting basalt slabs was probably associated with some kind of water-lustration ritual. This entire complex may represent what the Bible calls a *beit-bamat*, or house of high places (1 Kings 12:31).

It is possible that Jeroboam chose the northern flank of Tel Dan for the site of the royal *bamah* because of its proximity to the spring that serves as one of the

sources of the Jordan River. Jeroboam, however, may have chosen the site because it was traditionally hallowed as a cult site. Our finds here included two Egyptian cult fragments: The first depicts a person sitting cross-legged with the position of his hands suggestive of prayer; the second mentions the god Amun. Dating to the second millennium B.C.E., a figurine of a goddess adorned with an Egyptian-style wig was also found here. These finds suggest that the *bamah* was built on the site of an earlier sanctuary.

The royal *bamah* at Dan was enlarged in the centuries following Jeroboam's reign. Dating to the days of King Ahab—the first half of the ninth century B.C.E.—an almost square ashlar *bamah* measuring 60 by 62 feet has been uncovered. The *bamah* features an alternating series of headers (rectangular stones set with their ends parallel to the face of the platform) and stretchers (stones set with their ends perpendicular to the platform's face). There is evidence to suggest that a row of cedar beams was inserted between the rows of stones, as was done in the construction of the Temple of Jerusalem (1 Kings 6:36 and 1 Kings 7:12). A small four-horned altar and a large basalt horn, which must have originally been a corner of an extremely large altar designated for animal sacrifices, were also found.

The grandeur of the sanctuary in the eighth century B.C.E. is evident from the remains dating to the reign of Jeroboam II (784-748 B.C.E.). New steps leading up the *bamah* platform were constructed. Also associated with the *bamah* at this time were two long rooms that we call *leshakot* ("offices"; singular, *lishkah*), chambers that the Bible seems to associate with religious structures such as the Jerusalem Temple (see Ezra 8:29 and 1 Chronicles 9:26, among other passages). Inside the back room of one *lishkah* we found a low stone altar. Next to the altar, lying on the floor, were two long-handled iron shovels (a third lay nearby) used for coal. In the Bible, these shovels are called *machtot* (singular, *machtah*); see, for example, Leviticus 10:1. We also found a jar full of ashes, two incense altars and a bronze scepter head. All of these elements point to the importance of this shrine to the Dan community at a time when the eighth-century B.C.E. prophet Amos castigated the people for saying, "Thy god, O Dan, liveth" (Amos 8:14). A bilingual inscription in Greek and Aramaic referring to "the god who is in Dan" confirms the identification of the site as well as the existence of the shrine throughout the Hellenistic period (the third to the beginning of the first century B.C.E.).

If this were the only shrine at Dan, it would still be remarkable. Yet we have found a number of other religious installations at Dan during 31 years of digging, the longest-running excavation in all of Israel. (Why have so many shrines been found here? If other sites in Israel were as extensively excavated, would they too yield as many shrines?) The *bamah* just described is located well inside the city. Several others are clus-

DURING THE REIGN OF KING JEROBOAM II in the eighth century B.C.E., the royal *bamah* continued to flourish as a place of worship. Biran discovered two long chambers, called *leshakot* ("offices"; singular, *lishkah*), that date to this period. One *lishkah* contained a stone altar and a number of artifacts associated with it: a jar filled with ashes, two incense altars, a bronze scepter head and three iron shovels (right) used to scoop coals. Biran has identified the shovels, which measure a little over 2 feet long, as Biblical *machtot* (singular, *machtah*). Similar shovels, although with shorter handles, are depicted in synagogue mosaics dating to the Roman and Byzantine periods.

But the royal *bamah* is not the only shrine at Dan. Near the city's upper gate, Biran excavated a large structure (below) containing a limestone ashlar block broken in half, bearing a rectangular depression. The block was probably associated with a libation ceremony of some sort. Found near the lower gate, a stone (upper left) with a circular depression and a groove leading from edge to edge was also probably used in a libation ritual.

tered around the city's gate complex.

Approaching from the south, a beautifully paved road leads into Tel Dan. As you near the city gate, you cross a large paved plaza leading to the city's outer gate. Inside, you find yourself in another paved plaza with an inner gate that leads up to the city on the crest of the tell.

Early in our excavations of the Israelite fortifications, we discovered between the outer and inner gates a canopied throne-like dais (a raised platform) built of hewn limestone blocks (see plan, pp. 96-97). We knew it had been canopied since we discovered four round-socketed bases into which the poles supporting the canopy could be inserted. What was once under the canopy? we naturally wondered. The king? A statue of a deity? Next to this installation stood a large basalt monolith. Should we interpret this as a *maṣṣebah*, a standing stone that perhaps symbolizes a deity?

Many excavation seasons later, we were removing collapsed debris of the city wall, which the Assyrian king Tiglath-pileser III destroyed in the eighth century B.C.E. On the paved square between the inner and

SACRED STONES

Avraham Biran and his team have uncovered several shrines at Dan in addition to the large open-air *bamah* (high place) near the source of the Jordan River. Unlike that royal *bamah*, these shrines contain striking monoliths called *maṣṣebot,* or sacred pillars.

While clearing the fallen debris of the city wall between the outer and inner gates, which Tiglath-pileser III destroyed in 733/32 B.C.E. during his assault on Israel, Biran found a set of five standing stones (labeled number 3) bordering the wall. Votive vessels, seven-wick oil lamps, incense bowls and the bones of sacrificed animals found in the vicinity convinced Biran that the monoliths were indeed *maṣṣebot.*

About 125 feet east of Dan's outer gate, Biran found another set of five standing stones (labeled number 4) abutting the foot of the city wall, and yet another set of *maṣṣebot* (labeled number 2) was discovered just in front of the city's upper gate.

On the accumulated debris of the Assyrian destruction, about 60 feet from the city's outer gate, Biran discovered three, perhaps four, monoliths identified as *maṣṣebot* (labeled number 1). Set in front of the largest stone was a basalt bowl resting on a flattened base and filled with ashes. Two miniature jugs and three oil lamps found nearby indicated that the monoliths marked a place of cultic worship.

That so many *maṣṣebot* shrines are associated with Dan's gate complex suggests that these shrines were used by merchants or travelers, as well as by Dan's permanent residents, as they entered or left the city. It is possible that these structures are similar to those destroyed by King Josiah of Judah in the seventh century B.C.E. as a consequence of his religious reforms (see 2 Kings 23:8).

inner

paved pla.

paved pla

hussot

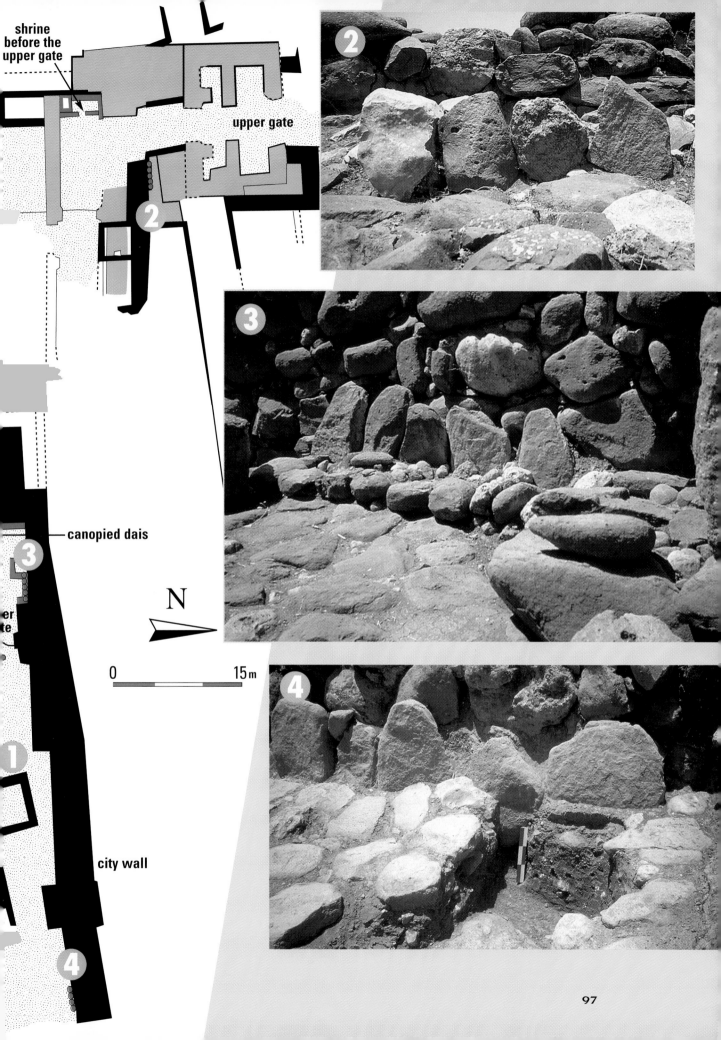

shrine
before the
upper gate

upper gate

2

canopied dais

3

N

0   15 m

1

city wall

4

outer city gates, we discovered five standing stones abutting the city wall (labeled number 3 on the plan, pp. 96-97). The stones are basalt monoliths of different sizes. In front of them was a bench or table.* At the western end of the line of stones was a single large stone that created a kind of niche for the standing stones. That these are *maṣṣebot*, or sacred pillars, there is no question: Nearby we found a variety of votive vessels including seven-wick oil lamps and incense bowls. Sheep and goat bones, also nearby, showed that sacrificed animals had been offered or eaten here.

These five standing stones, clearly *maṣṣebot*, suggested that the monolith we had discovered near the canopied dais was also a *maṣṣebah*. The canopied dais and the five nearby *maṣṣebot* were part of the same shrine located in the plaza between the outer and inner city gates.

At the end of the seventh century B.C.E., King Josiah of Judah enforced an important religious reform resulting in the condemnation of all shrines outside of Jerusalem and the destruction of the "high places (*bamot*) of the gates" (2 Kings 23:8). The complex between the inner and outer city gates of Dan may well represent archaeological evidence of "a high place of the gate."

We discovered two more sets of five standing stones (*maṣṣebot*) in the vicinity of the gate. One is located outside the outer gate, where we traced the city wall eastward for about 125 feet. Here, at the foot of the city wall, were five more standing stones carefully set on a solid foundation (number 4 on the plan). The

*See "'David' Found at Dan," **BAR**, March/April 1994.

BAZAAR RELIGION. What accounts for the large number of *maṣṣebot* shrines found apart from the large royal shrine located near the Jordan River? Biran suggests that they may have been set up to serve the religious needs of Dan's residents as well as those of merchants and travelers passing through the city. Biran has excavated a large building complex and shrine (above) located outside the city wall, about 80 feet from the outer gate. It is possible that this complex served as a religious shelter for people entering the city. Biran calls the structures of this complex *huṣṣot*, a word that in the Bible refers to streets or bazaars. The etymology of the word *huṣṣot* (from the Hebrew *huṣ*, meaning outside) suggests that these bazaars, like the structures shown above, were located outside a city's walls.

flat stones of the pavement were meticulously laid against the flat surfaces of the standing stones.

Then, in the course of excavating the paved road leading from the main gate to the crest of the site, we discovered still another shrine complex before the city's upper gate. In many ways it was like the shrine with the canopied dais between the inner and outer city gates. To the left (west) of the approach to the upper gate is a 15- by 8-foot structure with a dais on its left. Inside the structure was a limestone ashlar block broken in two. When we turned it over, we found a rectangular depression carved into it and a groove leading from the depression to the edge of the stone. It was apparently used in some kind of libation ceremony.

To the right (east) of the upper gate, set on a stone construction, were, once again, five stones, four standing and one fallen—another set of *maṣṣebot* constituting a "high place of the gate" (number 2 on the plan).

All of the shrines we have described so far date to no later than the middle of the eighth century B.C.E. In 733/32 B.C.E. the Assyrians under Tiglath-pileser III attacked Israel. Although Assyrian records do not mention Dan as one of the cities conquered or destroyed, it appears that Tiglath-pileser stopped by long enough to destroy the city's defenses. The gate area and the city wall were destroyed, but the city itself was spared, probably because it was not on the direct route to Hazor and Megiddo. Apparently Tiglath-pileser thought it was enough simply to destroy Dan's defenses.

The city continued to thrive, however, and actually reached its zenith in the seventh century B.C.E. The approach to the city remained in the south, and here, once again, a *maṣṣebot* shrine was built (number 1 on the plan). On the accumulated debris and collapsed stones along the city wall, 60 feet from the threshold of the outer Israelite gate and 10 feet south of the wall, three, possibly four, basalt standing monoliths identified as *maṣṣebot* were found. In front of the largest *maṣṣebah*, we found a basalt bowl on a carved stone, set on a flat base. The bowl was full of ashes. Close to the *maṣṣebot* in the back, we found two small juglets and three broken oil lamps—objects perhaps associated with cult practices at the shrine. Although the city gates and walls were still in ruins, the religious practices hallowed in previous generations obviously persisted.

THE GOD WHO IS IN DAN. Discovered in 1976 at the royal *bamah*, this stone bearing an inscription incised in Greek and Aramaic confirms the identity of Tel Dan. The inscription, which dates to the first half of the second century B.C.E., contains three lines of Greek and one line of Aramaic. The Greek text proclaims that a man named Zoilos offered a vow "to the god who is in Dan." The one line of Aramaic text is more puzzling, since a few letters are missing from the beginning and end of the line. Most probably, the line reads: "In Dan Zilas [the Aramaic version of Zoilos] made a vow to the god." The inscription confirms that the royal *bamah* of Jeroboam's time served as a sanctuary well into the Hellenistic period.

This was true also of the large royal shrine near the source of the Jordan River. But this raises another question. I have described a relatively large number of *maṣṣebot*; more have been found here than at probably any other site in Israel. Yet we have not discovered any at the city's major shrine at the Jordan River source. Why not? Negative evidence, of course, is not conclusive. Perhaps *maṣṣebot* do exist there, awaiting excavation. Or perhaps the *maṣṣebot* shrines we have described represent religion of a more popular character. Perhaps at the large royal shrine near the Jordan less elevated symbols of the deity were unnecessary. Although we can consider *maṣṣebot* as aniconic representations of the deity and an aspect of popular religion, they are, at Dan, quite distinct from the formal, royal rituals practiced at the same time at the royal shrine by the source of the Jordan.

If so, what of the *maṣṣebot* shrines elsewhere at Dan? Could these have been created for merchants and travelers, many of whom were not indigenous inhabitants of Dan? This possibility is not as far-fetched as it might seem. Outside the city wall, about 80 feet from the outer gate, we found an unusual building complex dating to the period before the destruction of Tiglath-pileser. Since this building complex was located beyond the city fortifications, we called these well-planned structures *huṣṣot*, from the Hebrew *huṣ*, which means outside. The term *huṣṣot*, appears many times in the Bible and is loosely translated as "streets" or "bazaars," which are not necessarily found outside a city gate. But the etymology of the word indicates that *huṣṣot*, like our structures, were often located outside city walls. At Dan these structures may have served as headquarters for the guards securing the entrance to the city. But it is also possible that they provided temporary shelter for people whose entrance to the city was delayed for some reason. To meet their religious needs, as well as those of inhabitants entering and leaving the city, the shrines at the gates were erected. That this practice was well entrenched is indicated by the fact that the best-preserved *maṣṣebot* shrine at Dan is the one built after Tiglath-pileser's destruction of the gates and city wall.

One final puzzle: The Bible refers only once to the *bamot* of the gate, yet as we have seen, Dan had more than one near the gates. Perhaps as more city gates from antiquity are excavated, other *bamot/maṣṣebot* shrines near city gates will come to light. ◘

Uncredited photos courtesy of the author.

CHAPTER EIGHT

Avraham Biran knows how to tell a story. In the introduction to his popular book on Dan, he promises to describe the site, not according to the chronological order of his discoveries, but in the order that history unfolded at Dan throughout the ages. Thus his book begins, "In the beginning there was only water." As the waters of the prehistoric sea recede to reveal the region known as the Galilee and the Golan Heights, we embark on his story of Dan.

In this chapter, our reviewer praises the book but calls for a more detailed report written for professional archaeologists. The call was answered in 1996 with the publication of *Dan I: A Chronicle of the Excavations* (Jerusalem: Hebrew Union College–Jewish Institute of Religion), the first volume of the final scientific excavation report.

A Review of Biblical Dan

by Avraham Biran

(Jerusalem: Israel Exploration Society and Hebrew Union College/Jewish Institute of Religion, 1994)
Reviewed by John Laughlin

Avraham Biran's excavation of Tel Dan, begun in 1966, is the longest continuous excavation of any site in Israel. Located in a beautiful valley in northern Galilee, the tell has yielded an enormous amount of material spanning the Neolithic to the Late Roman periods—some five thousand years of occupational history. The excavator is the director of the Nelson Glueck School of Biblical Archaeology at the Hebrew Union College/Jewish Institute of Religion in Jerusalem and a former director of the Israel Department of Antiquities.

Although Biran has published numerous articles on various aspects of the excavation, this volume is his first book-length report on Dan. A revised English version of the author's original 1992 Hebrew edition, it is written in a popular, non-technical style intended for a general audience.

Biran describes the occupational history of the site, beginning with the Neolithic period (fifth millennium B.C.E.) and ending with a brief discussion of Dan's history from Iron Age II (1000 B.C.E.) through the Roman periods (first century B.C.E.-fourth century C.E.). In a postscript, the author relates the dramatic discovery of the now-famous Aramaic inscription found in July 1993.[1] The bulk of the book is devoted to the Middle Bronze Age (2200-1550 B.C.E.) and to what Biran calls "The Sacred Precinct," located in Area T.

In the Middle Bronze Age II period (c. 1900-1550 B.C.E.), Dan (then called Laish) was a thriving Canaanite city. During this time, the Canaanites built the huge earthen rampart that gives the mound its present shape. Biran suggests how this rampart was built, based on his excavations of it in four areas. He concludes that at its base the rampart was nearly 200 feet thick. Biran estimates that to construct the rampart would have required 1,000 workmen laboring for three years.

Associated with this massive rampart is the remarkable triple-arched gate, first discovered in 1979. Biran devotes an entire chapter to this impressive architectural remain, describing in detail its excavation and construction. The top plans and section drawings included in his discussion, as well as numerous photographs, make this chapter one of the more useful in the book. Unfortunately, the rapid deterioration of the sun-dried mudbrick of which the gate was constructed required that the gate be partially covered again in order to preserve it.

The longest chapter discusses the excavation of Area T, where this reviewer began his own archaeological field work in 1978. The discoveries here leave little doubt that this part of the site served as a religious center throughout most of Dan's long history. Biran restricts his discussion primarily to the Israelite phases to which most of the architectural remains were dated. The rich material found here includes altars, incense stands, statuary, faience figurines, numerous ceramic vessels (including seven-spouted oil lamps) and architectural remains. Among the latter is what Biran identifies as a *bamah* (often translated "high place";[2] see 1 Kings 12:31), the first phase of which he dates to the time of King Jeroboam I of the northern kingdom of Israel (tenth-ninth centuries B.C.E.).

Among the important discoveries at Tel Dan, the following are especially noteworthy. A bilingual Greek and Aramaic inscription containing a reference to "the god who is in Dan" was found in 1976. This inscription provides rare literary evidence for the identity of the site and for the cultic nature of this part of the tell.

In 1978 a plastered basin from the tenth-ninth centuries B.C.E. was found south of the *bamah*. A large basalt slab flanked each end of the basin. Attached to the end of each slab was a large sunken jar. Despite the superficial similarity between this structure and olive presses known from other excavations, Biran identifies it as some sort of a water libation installation.[3] Many archaeologists remain skeptical of this interpretation, preferring instead the olive-press explanation. To support his conclusion, Biran argues that because the bottom of the sunken basin is constructed of unplastered stones, any attempt to collect olive oil in it would have resulted in considerable waste of this valuable commodity. Whether or not it served for water libations is still uncertain.

A few meters southwest of the *bamah* lies a rectangular room that Biran dates to the eighth century B.C.E.[4] In this room Biran found a stone structure measuring 1.03 by 1.03 meters (3 feet, 3 inches square) and standing 27 centimeters (10.6 inches) high. Associated with this apparent altar were three iron shovels, a bronze bowl and part of a jar that had been buried in the ground upside down. The jar was full of ashes. Biran identified the stone structure as an altar from the time of Jeroboam II. Removal of the altar stones revealed a bronze and silver scepter head 9 centimeters (3.5 inches) high and 3.7 centimeters (1.5 inches) wide. Why this object was buried beneath the altar is still a mystery.[5]

The book is enhanced by a brief bibliography, 228 illustrations and 44 color plates. Informed readers interested in Biblical archaeology will find it useful for its broad description of this major Israelite tell. However, its lack of detailed stratigraphical section drawings and top plans (especially for Area T) showing precise relationships of artifacts to architectural phases will reduce the usefulness of Biran's book for other archaeologists. For their sake, we hope that more detailed reports will be published in the near future.

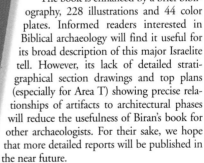

John Laughlin is chair of the Department of Religion, Averett College, Danville, Virginia.

[1] See "'David' Found at Dan," **BAR**, March/April 1994.

[2] See Beth Alpert Nakhai, "What's a Bamah?" **BAR**, May/June 1994.

[3] See "Is the Cultic Installation at Dan Really an Olive Press?" **BAR**, November/December 1984.

[4] See Hershel Shanks, "Avraham Biran—Twenty Years of Digging at Tel Dan," **BAR**, July/August 1987.

[5] See Avraham Biran, "Tel Dan Scepter Head," **BAR**, January/February 1989.

CHAPTER NINE

Avraham Biran's name will forever be linked with the dig at Tel Dan, the longest running excavation in Israel. His successes at Dan are even more astonishing, however, when we recall that this is only part of the archaeological work he has completed over the past 65 years. In the following pages, Biran describes one of his "smaller" projects—a mere seven years spent at Aroer, in the Negev.

Working with Rudolph Cohen of the Israel Department of Antiquities from 1975 to 1982, Biran revealed cities at Aroer dating from the seventh to sixth century B.C. as well as from the turn of the millennium. This small clay fertility figurine (opposite) dates to the earlier period. According to the Bible, however, there was an even earlier city of Aroer, in the days of David, but excavations revealed nothing from this period. In this chapter, Biran presents his work at Aroer as an example of how archaeology and the Bible can—and cannot—illuminate one another.

"And David Sent Spoils...to

EXCAVATORS BRING TO LIFE ANCIENT NEGEV FORTRESS

THREE SITES IN THE BIBLE—and perhaps four*—are called Aroer (pronounced *Ah-roe-air*). We call one Aroer of the Negev. The other two—or three—are east of the Jordan River.

Aroer may mean "crest of a mountain." This very general description would explain why several sites have this name. Or, Aroer may be derived from the name of the juniper plant, *Ar'ar (Juniperus Phoenicia)*, a common plant in arid zones; this meaning also could give rise to several Aroers.

The most frequently mentioned Aroer** is on the bank of the river known in the Bible as the Arnon (the Wadi Mujib). The Arnon was on the ancient route called the King's Highway on the high plateau east of the Jordan River. This Aroer marked the southern boundary of the Israelite territories in Transjordan and is even mentioned in line 26 of the famous Mesha stone.[1] A Spanish archaeological team excavated this Aroer in 1964-65.

The second Biblical Aroer† is located near ancient Amman, located at modern Amman, capital of Jordan. This Aroer was part of the territory of the tribe of Gad. Jephthah, one of the Israelite judges, fought the Ammonites "from Aroer to Minnith" (Judges 11:33). The exact identification of this Aroer is, however, uncertain, and it has never been excavated.

As for the third Aroer, we're really not sure it is mentioned in the Bible and whether, if it is, it might be the same as the second Aroer. The relevant passage in the Hebrew Bible, Isaiah 17:2, differs from that of the Septuagint, the third to first century B.C. Greek translation of the Hebrew Bible. (There are also differences among modern translations.) The chapter as a whole is a prophecy against Damascus: "Damascus shall cease to be a city; it shall become a heap of ruins." The Hebrew version con-

---

*Readers who remember Amos 1 will recognize this as a paraphrase.

**Joshua 12:2; 13:9, 16; Deuteronomy 2:36; 3:12; 4:48; 2 Kings 10:33; Jeremiah 48:19; Judges 11:26; 1 Chronicles 5:8.

†Numbers 32:34; Joshua 13:25; 2 Samuel 24:5.

A Bedouin woman *waters her flock. This well served the inhabitants of ancient Aroer just as it serves the Bedouin today.*

he Elders in Aroer" *(1 Samuel 30: 26–28)*

ut Find No Remains from David's Time

By Avraham Biran

"AND DAVID SENT SPOILS…"

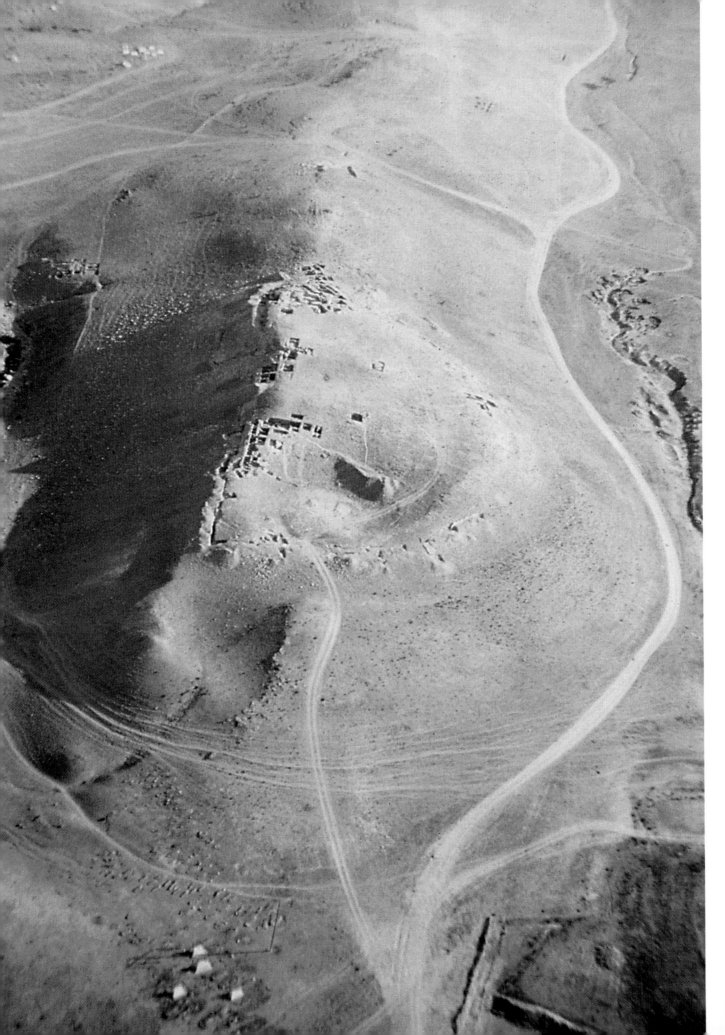

Aroer viewed from the air. *Wadis, or dry river beds, surround three sides of the five-acre site. In antiquity, this topographic feature afforded the town natural protection from attack.*

tinues, "The town of Aroer shall be deserted." In the Septuagint, the second verse reads, "Its towns shall be deserted forever"—but there is no mention of Aroer. Many modern translations accept the Septuagint version rather than the Hebrew version. But, obviously, this may—or may not—be a reference to a third Aroer, often called the Damascus Aroer. If it is a third Aroer, it may be the one cited in an extra-Biblical text from the eighth century B.C. first published in 1958.[2]

The fourth Aroer—or the third, depending on how you're counting—is mentioned only once in the Bible, in 1 Samuel 30:26-31.* This is the Aroer in the Negev of Israel—the Aroer we excavated between 1975 and 1981, and the one on which I would like to report to **BAR** readers.

When the future King David—and 600 of his men—fled from the wrath of King Saul and entered the service of the Philistine lord Achish of Gath, Achish granted David Ziklag to live in as his own city (1 Samuel 27). Later, the Amalekites raided and burned Ziklag while David and his men were away (1 Samuel 30). When David returned and found Ziklag destroyed, he pursued the Amalekites and defeated them and took much spoil. Although he was then in the service of the Philistines, David distributed the spoils to the elders of Judah saying, " 'This is a present for you from our spoil of the enemies of the Lord.' [David sent the spoil to the elders] in Bethel . . . and . . . in Aroer," (1 Samuel 30:26-28).

I never cease to marvel at the revelations of archaeology. How much of our knowledge of history depends on the archaeologist's spade. The Negev Aroer is surely a case in point. Except for the Biblical reference telling us that there were elders there in David's time, nothing at all is known of the place. These elders must have been important enough for David to seek their favor and thus win their support in his effort to consolidate the United Monarchy of Israel. But exactly where the Negev Aroer was and what kind of city it was, we are not told.

The Negev Aroer was identified in 1838 by that intrepid American scholar and traveler Edward Robinson, to whom we owe so much in our study of the historical geography of the Holy Land. In the Negev, Robinson found a broad *wadi*** with "many pits for water which are called Ar'arah and give the name to the valley . . . . In the valley and on the western hill are evident traces of an ancient village or town . . . . small fragments of pottery are also everywhere

visible. In this instance, the name leaves little room to doubt that this is the site of ancient Aroer of the south of Judah."[3]

This identification has now been universally accepted by Bible scholars as well as archaeologists. There can be no doubt that the Arabic names *Ar'arah* and *Bir Ar'air* ("wells of Aroer") represent the modern linguistic descendants of the Aroer of old.

Some of the ancient ways of life persist at this site. The Bedouin still bring their animals to be watered at the ancient wells. Neither the heavy traffic on the modern highway from Beersheba to Dimona nor the occasional train carrying phosphates from Oron disturbs the patriarchal scene—unchanged from time immemorial. As I watched the modern traffic and the patriarchal Bedouin on an early trip to the ruins of Aroer, I thought to myself, "Neither the drivers of camels nor the drivers of the cars, in the pursuit of their daily lives, are aware of the hidden treasures of ancient Aroer that they are passing."

Rudolph Cohen,[4] District Archaeologist of the Israel Department of Antiquities, and I directed the archaeological expedition of Hebrew Union College—Jewish Institute of Religion (HUC-JIR) to Aroer. Our purpose was not, however, to prove or disprove the existence of a city in David's time. The encroachments of modern civilization were endangering the ancient remains and we were asked to conduct a short emergency excavation that would uncover and preserve as much information as possible in a short period.

A preliminary survey of the site revealed that the remains of ancient occupation covered a relatively large area of over five acres. By comparison, the much more famous Beersheba, which is nearby, covered only two and one half acres.

In 1975, we mounted a brief two-week campaign. The rescue operation revealed remains of large buildings and a jar handle stamped with the letters *l m l k (lamelech)* meaning "belonging to the king." We also found a dome-shaped stone weight incised with the sign for four shekels, a small limestone altar, a sherd with the remains of three Hebrew letters, probably representing the word *shalosh* (three), a fragment of a glass bowl similar to those found in Assyrian palaces, and a stone silo containing a large number of vessels and an Astarte figurine. Further excavations were clearly in order. So each year until 1981, we returned to the

---

*It may however be referred to in Joshua 15:12 as Adadah, which the Septuagint renders as "Aruel."

**A *wadi* (Arabic) or *nahal* (Hebrew) is a dry river bed or small river common in Israel and the neighboring regions. During the rainy season, a wadi or nahal may become a raging torrent for a few hours, or even days, or it can be a relatively calm stream.

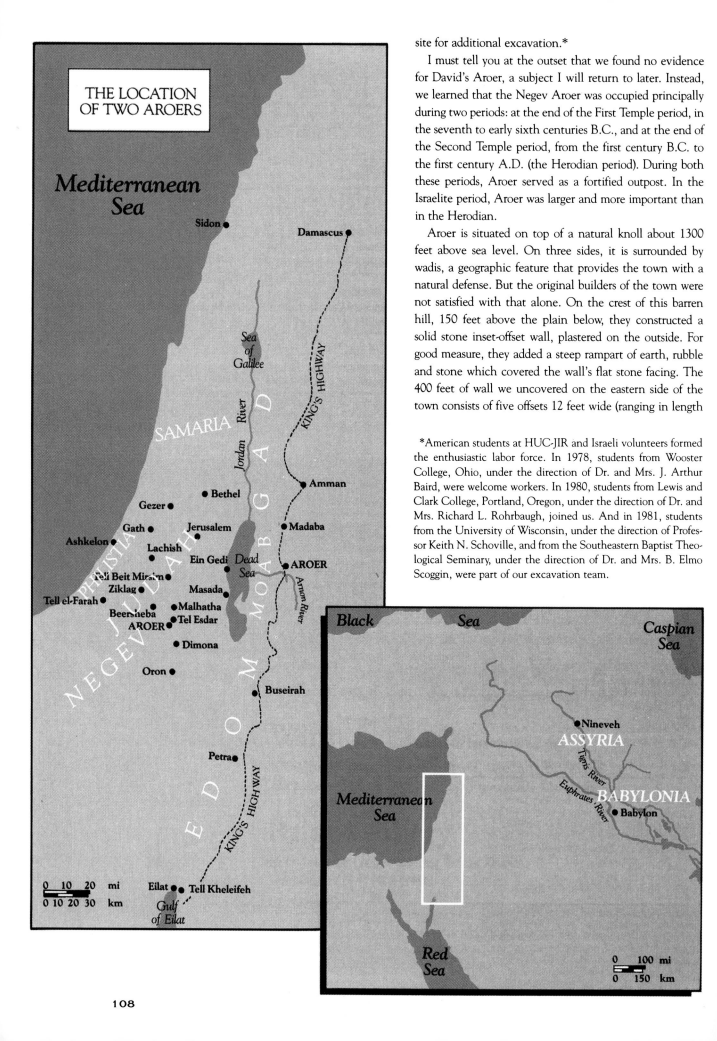

THE LOCATION OF TWO AROERS

Mediterranean Sea

Sidon

Damascus

SAMARIA

Sea of Galilee

KING'S HIGHWAY

Jordan River

G A D

Bethel

Gezer

Amman

Gath

Jerusalem

Madaba

Ashkelon

Lachish

AROER

PHILISTIA

Ein Gedi

Dead Sea

Tell Beit Mirsim

Masada

Arnon River

Ziklag

JUDAH

Tell el-Farah

Malhatha

Beersheba

AROER

Tel Esdar

NEGEV

Dimona

E D O M

M O A B

Oron

Buseirah

Petra

KING'S HIGHWAY

0 10 20 mi
0 10 20 30 km

Eilat Tell Kheleifeh

Gulf of Eilat

Black   Sea

Caspian Sea

Nineveh

ASSYRIA

Tigris River

Euphrates River

BABYLONIA

Mediterranean Sea

Babylon

Red Sea

0   100 mi
0   150 km

site for additional excavation.*

I must tell you at the outset that we found no evidence for David's Aroer, a subject I will return to later. Instead, we learned that the Negev Aroer was occupied principally during two periods: at the end of the First Temple period, in the seventh to early sixth centuries B.C., and at the end of the Second Temple period, from the first century B.C. to the first century A.D. (the Herodian period). During both these periods, Aroer served as a fortified outpost. In the Israelite period, Aroer was larger and more important than in the Herodian.

Aroer is situated on top of a natural knoll about 1300 feet above sea level. On three sides, it is surrounded by wadis, a geographic feature that provides the town with a natural defense. But the original builders of the town were not satisfied with that alone. On the crest of this barren hill, 150 feet above the plain below, they constructed a solid stone inset-offset wall, plastered on the outside. For good measure, they added a steep rampart of earth, rubble and stone which covered the wall's flat stone facing. The 400 feet of wall we uncovered on the eastern side of the town consists of five offsets 12 feet wide (ranging in length

*American students at HUC-JIR and Israeli volunteers formed the enthusiastic labor force. In 1978, students from Wooster College, Ohio, under the direction of Dr. and Mrs. J. Arthur Baird, were welcome workers. In 1980, students from Lewis and Clark College, Portland, Oregon, under the direction of Dr. and Mrs. Richard L. Rohrbaugh, joined us. And in 1981, students from the University of Wisconsin, under the direction of Professor Keith N. Schoville, and from the Southeastern Baptist Theological Seminary, under the direction of Dr. and Mrs. B. Elmo Scoggin, were part of our excavation team.

from 37 feet to 45 feet), and four insets 6 feet to 7 feet wide (ranging in length from 42 feet to 50 feet). This wall enclosed an area of 2.5 acres, but people also lived on another 2.5 acres outside the wall.

We excavated a number of rooms built against the inner face of the wall. To overcome the steep natural slope of the hill and to obtain a horizontal level for the floors, the builders had first laid a layer of pebbles. This was a sensible solution to a difficult topographical problem. Once a fairly livable surfce was created, a layer of ash and a floor of beaten earth was added.

This was the first settlement at Aroer, what we called stratum III—the third level down from the top. We reached this level in some places in our first two-week excavation. At that time we also found the stone silo to which I referred earlier. It was built on bedrock. The assemblage of finds it contained was obviously of the same period as our stratum III residential structures. If we could date this assemblage, we could date the founding of Aroer.

Some of the vessels from the silo were similar to vessels found in the destruction level of the city of Lachish, destroyed by Sennacherib in 701 B.C (Lachish III). However, on the basis of other comparisons, a number of our vessels were clearly datable to the seventh century B.C., and not earlier. Obviously, despite the devastation of this part of Judah by Sennacherib's Assyrian army in 701 B.C., the population had not been totally annihilated. Potters and other artisans continued to practice their trade, as this pottery demonstrated. Moreover, pottery forms and textures of the eighth century did not disappear. Instead they continued to be used even though new forms and new vessels were also introduced.

The date of our pottery assemblage from the silo must be determined not by the earlier eighth century vessels but by the new vessels that appeared only in the seventh century B.C. In subsequent seasons we found more vessels from the seventh century B.C. in rooms built on virgin soil, both inside and outside the town wall. The conclusion is clear—Aroer was first settled in the seventh century B.C. after Sennacherib destroyed the surrounding area at the end of the eighth century (701 B.C.).

This is not as radical a conclusion as it may seem. Archaeological surveys and excavations in the Judean mountains and hills and in the Negev have recently revealed intensive settlement in the seventh century B.C. This unprecedented increase in settlements in the southern kingdom of Judah may have been the result of a population influx from Samaria following the Assyrian conquest of the northern kingdom of Israel in 721 B.C.

Who built Aroer? We can propose two candidates. One is King Manasseh, who ruled for 55 years in the seventh century, the longest reign of any king of Judah. In that century, after Sennacherib's campaign, Judah was vassal to Assyria. But perhaps Manasseh took advantage of the unsettled conditions in the Assyrian Empire that preceded and followed the Babylonian revolt to strengthen the boundaries of his Judean kingdom. Perhaps Manasseh built Aroer as a bulwark against attack from the south. Although the Bible does not speak well of Manasseh, he must nevertheless be given credit for fortifying Jerusalem and for putting "military commanders in all the walled cities of Judah" (2 Chronicles 33:14). Perhaps Aroer was one of these walled cities.

Another possibility must also be considered. Aroer may have been built by King Hezekiah, who reigned during Sennacherib's campaign. Sennacherib besieged Jerusalem, but was unable to take the city. According to the Bible, after the Lord slew 185,000 Assyrian soldiers in a single night (2 Kings 19:35), Sennacherib withdrew and Jerusalem was saved. The respite given Hezekiah after Sennacherib withdrew from Jerusalem may have prompted the Judean king to fortify his southern border, including the building of Aroer. In that case, Aroer would already have been a walled city when Manasseh became king. The Biblical reference to Manasseh placing military commanders in all the walled cities of Judah would then mean that he placed a military commander in Aroer, but he did not build it.

We do not know how long the first settlement at Aroer lasted. But the fact that no gap exists between the earliest stratum, Aroer III, and Aroer II suggests that this first settlement was not completely destroyed. The walls of Aroer III houses continued in use in Aroer II, with additions and repairs. Although a thin layer of ash separates the two strata, this layer is far different from the thick ash layer that represents the total destruction of Lachish III. The thin ash layer at Aroer suggests that the destruction was the result of local skirmishes and attacks in the seventh to sixth centuries B.C. In any event, Aroer was soon rebuilt after the misfortunes that befell stratum III.

Stratum II at Aroer represents a large and prosperous community. Whether the original city wall continued to serve as the main defense has not been determined. The date of Aroer II can easily be determined. The pottery repertoire is similar to that found at Ein Gedi, Lachish II, Tell Beit Mirsim, Jerusalem and many other sites, dating to the end of the Iron Age, the late seventh to early sixth centuries B.C. No doubt Aroer was destroyed, along with these other cities and hamlets of Judah, when Nebuchadnezzar, king of Babylon, conquered Judah and destroyed Jerusalem in 587-6 B.C.

Aroer II probably existed for about 30 or 40 years. Perhaps it was built by King Josiah who introduced the religious reformation associated with the composition of Deuteronomy.

Despite the fact that Aroer II lasted only about 30 to 40 years, it included three to five phases of occupation. It is as though houses had been destroyed and rebuilt, floor levels raised, walls reused, and household installations built one on top of the other—all within one generation.

This must have been a period of great prosperity. In addition to the evidence of continual building and rebuilding, we found a large assemblage of fine pottery. Even more important were the finds pointing to strong cultural and commercial ties with the maritime coast to the west and with the land of Edom across the Jordan River in the east. This should come as no surprise, because Aroer was located on an important Negev trade route. Decorated "Edomite" sherds of fine texture, similar to those found in Buseirah (Biblical Bozrah) in Edom, were uncovered in almost all excavation areas. A cone-shaped jasper seal is further evidence for an Edomite connection. It was pierced horizontally to be worn on a string. The seal was inscribed *l q o s a*, belonging to Qosa. Qos was an Edomite deity. The owner of this seal thus had a name that included the name of an Edomite deity. Names with the component Qos are known from Assyrian records. Qosgabr, for example, was a king of Edom in the seventh century; the name Qosanal was found on seal impressions on seventh century jars at Tell Kheleifeh near Eilat.

We believe that Aroer was the main administrative center in the southern part of Judah, just before the Babylonian conquest. Edom was Judah's neighbor on the east. When they were not fighting each other, Edom and Judah must have had extensive commercial and cultural ties.

Aroer's cultural affinities also extended westward to the Mediterranean coast, as evidenced by the Assyrian Palace Ware vessels we found. We also found a finely polished bone plaque (see p. 113), two inches by one inch, that may have come from the coast and was perhaps influenced by Phoenician culture. We think this plaque may be a calendar. There are three rows of ten holes each (30 days?) and a fourth row with 12 holes (12 months?). Other similar rectangular bone objects with holes have been found at other sites such as Gezer, Lachish and Tell el-Farah (south), but they have only three rows of ten holes each. Ours has four rows with a total of 42 holes. Perhaps a moveable peg was inserted in each hole or groove to mark the days of the month. Our plaque is also unique because the top is in the shape of a proto-Aeolian capital with three additional holes. If our suggestion that this is a calendar is correct, the three top holes may denote some division of the year.

The inhabitants of Aroer must have had a special affection for the goddess of fecundity. Five intact Astarte figurines and fragments of others were found in various areas of the excavations. We also found three small household

Stone silo *built on bedrock. Fragments of seventh-century B.C. storage jars found undisturbed in this silo fix the date of the earliest settlement at Aroer.*

incense altars; whether they are related to the Astarte cult we cannot say.

But what of the Aroer from David's time, referred to in the first book of Samuel? If the Aroer to which David sent part of the spoils of his war with the Amalekites has not been found in our excavations, where is it? Although we reached virgin soil in all excavated areas and found no evidence whatever for an 11th to 10th century B.C. settlement, it is always possible that somewhere on this five-acre site, early remains may yet be found. However, this is unlikely. A better theory is that the location of Davidic Aroer is at a site called Tel Esdar, about a mile and a half north of Aroer. Tel Esdar was excavated in 1963-64 when the railway to Dimona threatened it. The expedition uncovered remains from the 11th to 10th centuries B.C., indicating that the town was of some importance in the Davidic period. Tel Esdar was abandoned in the 10th century B.C., possibly because it had been built on the plain and was therefore indefensible. Perhaps the name Aroer did not disappear, and when, in the seventh century B.C., a fortified city was built in a more defensible location on a knoll nearby, the old name was given to the new site. The transfer of a name from one location to another was a well-known practice in antiquity and may explain the absence of 11th to 10th century remains precisely at the Aroer we excavated.

What happened to our Aroer after the destruction of stratum II is also unclear. Apparently, the site was unoccupied for about 500 years following the Babylonian destruction of the last Israelite settlement of stratum II.* Then a new town was built on the hill.

This new town had a large central courtyard (150 feet by 110 feet) and a fortress on the southeast corner of the mound. Commanding the site as well as the entire area below it to the south, this fortress is an impressive structure, built of large limestone blocks beautifully worked in the center-boss style associated with the Herodian period (see p. 113). The fortress is almost square (38 feet by 35 feet). Some of its walls are preserved to a height of six courses (eight feet) above the stone-paved floor of the ground level, which was divided into four inter-connecting rooms by two intersecting internal walls.

The original height of the fortress is unknown. All inner

*We did find a Rhodian jar handle, a few Hellenistic sherds and two coins of Antiochus III (233 B.C.-187 B.C.), indicating that some activity may have taken place at the site in the third to the first centuries B.C. However, no architectural remains were found.

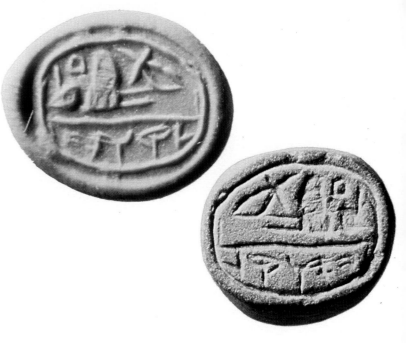

Jasper seal *(above). On the left, a wax impression of the seal allows us to read the mirror-image inscription appearing on the actual seal. The inscription reads lqosa, belonging to Qosa. Qos, a component of this name, was an Edomite deity. In the late seventh to early sixth centuries B.C., Aroer was a prosperous community, trading actively with settlements in the land of Edom across the Jordan River, so the seal may have come from Edomite territory.*

Four-shekel weight. *This dome-shaped object is incised with two symbols—the number four at left (which looks like a modern number seven) and the sign for shekel at right. Originally, the word shekel denoted a unit of weight; at later times, and in Israel today, it refers to a monetary denomination.*

Glass fragment. *Originally part of a bowl, this fragment resembles very rare Assyrian luxury glass from the eighth to seventh centuries B.C., found in Shalmaneser's palace in Nimrud.*

and outer walls are of uniform width, four feet, and their inner openings are uniformly narrow, two and one half feet, and eight feet high, giving a firm structural potential for a much greater height and additional upper floors. It is safe to assume that the fortress was at least two stories high. A section about three feet deep in the northwestern corner revealed that the floor was built on a stone fill, which may represent an earlier Iron Age fortress.

The fortress building was itself part of a larger courtyard/garrison complex located on the inner face of the old Israelite city wall. In houses and rooms of the Herodian period along the courtyard wall, we found a destruction level con-

Astarte, goddess of fertility. *A number of fragments like the heads at left were found at Aroer, all dating from the late seventh to early sixth centuries B.C. The Astarte (top), wearing a pointed hat, was made in a mold. Some paint on the figure is preserved—yellow on her hair, red on her forehead and face, and black outlining her eyes and accenting her eyebrows.*

Limestone altar *for burning incense or spices. Almost square, this altar measures 2.5 inches long, 2.3 inches wide and two inches high.*

taining charred remains of wooden beams, a bronze mirror, a bronze bell, a juglet, oil lamps, glass fragments, Nabatean sherds, and a coin of the Procurator Antonius Felix from the year 59 A.D.

South of the courtyard wall, we excavated two Herodian rooms in which we uncovered storage jars, measuring cups, oil lamps and glass fragments. One of the glass fragments is of a type known as a "Sidonian" glass cup. Three Greek leters, "AXA," can be seen on it; they are part of the word [KAT] AXA [IRE], meaning jubilation. Thus the cup was probably used for celebrations or for blessings.

Apparently there was only one access to the fortress. This principle of limited and guarded access was emphasized by the fact that a plastered stone girdle six to seven feet wide was built against all four walls of the fortress. On the courtyard corner, at the fortress entrance, the fortress wall was also reinforced on the inside.

We are not sure who built this fortress and the associated settlement. Most likely they were built by Herod the Great in the second half of the first century B.C. during his extensive building activities, especially at Masada. However, no Herodian coins have been found at Aroer. Another, less likely, possibility is Herod Agrippa (41-44 A.D.). The fact that we found coins minted by Agrippa supports this possibility. (We also found other coins from

Coin of the First Jewish Revolt. *The fluted amphora with brim and two handles at the right of the coin is encircled by the Hebrew inscription,* shnat shtayim, *meaning "year two" (67/68 A.D.) of the Jewish revolt against Rome. Two of these coins were found at Aroer, along with a mass of stone rubble, strong evidence that the Romans devastated the military outpost of Aroer in about 68 A.D.*

Aroer fortress wall. *The fine workmanship and center-boss style of this masonry help identify it as the work of Herod the Great. Here, parts of three courses are visible; in some places, six courses (eight feet high) were preserved. Each course is four feet deep—ample thickness for a wall supporting more than one story.*

Seventh-century calendar? *(below) This smooth bone plaque measures just over two inches long and one inch wide. Perhaps a peg was moved each day of the month from one to the next of the 30 holes arranged in three rows of ten holes each. In the fourth row of 12 holes, another peg might have been moved to mark off the completion of each month. Scholars are not sure, however, that the plaque is a calendar.*

Although similar plaques with holes have been found at other sites in Israel, only this one is topped with the form of a proto-Aeolic capital.

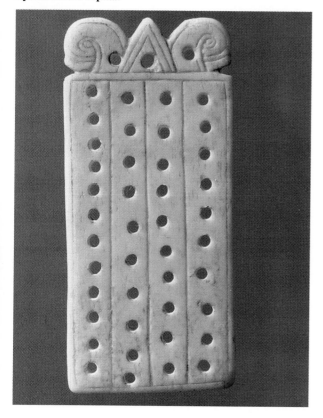

about the same period; one minted in Ashkelon in about 40 A.D. depicts the Roman Emperor Caligula). Josephus, who wrote extensively about the hisory of the land in the last decades before the Roman destruction of the Temple in 70 A.D., says that Agrippa owned a *pyrgos*, or stronghold at Malhatha, which is identified with Tel Malhata about seven miles north of Aroer. Agrippa's domain probably extended as far as Aroer, so he could have built a fortress here—or enlarged and strengthened an existing one.

The fortress may have been strengthened again just before the first Jewish revolt against Rome (66-70 A.D.). Because of its wells, Aroer may have served as the Negev headquarters of the Jewish revolutionary commander Simon Bar Giora. Among the finds were two coins from the second year of the Jewish revolt. On the obverse of the coins is an amphora framed with a Hebrew inscription, *Shnat shtayim* (year two). On the reverse is a leaf from a grapevine and another Hebrew inscription *leherut zion* (for the freedom of Zion). These coins and the mass of fallen stones provide the archaeological evidence for the Roman destruction of Aroer about the year 70 A.D., in the course of the suppression of the Jewish revolt.

All photographs in this article © Hebrew Union College-Jewish Institute of Religion.

[1]See Dan Cole's review of *Digging for God and Country,* by Neil Asher Silberman, **BAR**, July/August 1982, p. 10.

[2]See A. Dupont-Sommer, *Les Inscriptions Araméennes de Sfiré* (Paris: 1958), and B. Mazar, "The Aramean Empire and its Relations with Israel," *Biblical Archeologist* Vol. 25, (1962), p. 118.

[3]Edward Robinson, *Biblical Researches in Palestine, Mount Sinai and Arabia Petraea.* London, 1841.

[4]Rudolph Cohen is familiar to **BAR** readers as the author of "Did I Excavate Kadesh-Barnea?" May/June 1981, and "The Marvelous Mosaics of Kissufim," January/February 1980.